A
Celebration
of Life

Catholic Spirituality Today

Anthony T. Padovano

Resurrection Press
Mineola, New York

Front cover design: Tom Grasso

Copyright © 1990 by Dr. Anthony T. Padovano

First published in 1990 by   Resurrection Press
P.O. Box 248
Williston Park, NY 11596

Second printing — June 1992

ISBN 0-9623410-9-6

Library of Congress Catalog Card Number 90-061563

Printed in the United States of America by Faith Printing.

Contents

Introduction

1. Summons to Life 1
2. Contemplation 13
3. Love 23
4. Sacrament 31
5. Church . . . . , , , , , , , ... 37
6. Failure 47
7. Recovery 59
8. Suffering 69
9. Healing 79
10. Community 89
11. Christ 97
12. Gratitude and Grace 107

Introduction

Spirituality is not an addition to life which each of us might gain or lose with little consequence.

It is not something limited in its significance to people in religious institutions.

It is an inescapable and urgent concern of every person, whether that person would recognize the word "spirituality" or not.

Spirituality has something to do with the spirit of one's life, with the environment or atmosphere in which one lives, with the kind of world we choose to inhabit.

Spirituality, quite simply, is about meaning and purpose, about whether we count or are accountable, about whether we make a difference or live without significance.

And so, we must settle early on in our minds and hearts questions about spirituality and meaning. There is too much at issue in these things for us to ignore them.

~~~~~~~~~

One of the oldest metaphors about life is the journey. This book intends to take you on a journey, one in which meaning and spirituality will be explored. You, the reader, are the central figure in this book. The hopes of this book are your hopes. The ultimate achievement of this book is the sense of accomplishment which you perceive with your own life.

A journey is easier if one has a companion. This book is company for the journey, a friend one might turn to, a help in the dialogue each of us conducts with oneself and others about the point and purpose of it all.

If this book succeeds, it will lead us to become companions of others who might otherwise have travelled with greater burdens, missing the mark or giving up in despair and exhaustion because the journey seemed impossible or, at the very least, lonely and pointless.

Chapter One

Summons to Life

There is an unfortunate tendency in the Catholic community to identify the word "vocation" exclusively with people who live as celibates in a formal and canonical religious community approved by Church leaders and carefully supervised by them.

For most Catholics, the word "vocation" has something to do with monks and nuns, with priests and religious sisters or brothers. Such people, indeed, have a vocation but the term has wider and richer applications than this limited usage.

A vocation is a call from God, a summons or a destiny to live a particular lifestyle in accord with the Gospel or with all that is best in us.

Perhaps some examples may help before we explain the definition of vocation further.

Most Catholics do not see their marriages as vocations. If a priest at a liturgy asks us to pray for vocations, most Catholics would think of formal religious community life. Few would pray that God might call people to marriages which are in accord with the Gospel or with all that is best in them.

For most Catholics, a prayer for vocations does not include, as it should, a prayer for people who choose to live a single life or for a life in widowhood, for people who choose to live a life of service to humanity or for people who live out their careers with decency and love.

If we wish to pray for vocations to formal religious community, we should say this explicitly. There should be other prayers, however, for people in other vocations and lifestyles in the Church and in the world.

If a young woman is preparing to become a religious sister and then decides to become a married woman instead, many Catholics might regard her as someone who did not follow a vocation. In reality, her situation ought to be described differently. She is a woman who thought she had a vocation to formal religious community life and pursued this diligently and generously. She discovered in the course of preparation that God had given her an equally valid vocation as a married woman.

She did not "lose" a vocation. Quite the opposite. She found a vocation and followed it. And it was not a lesser vocation or one that, in itself, is less involved with God or Church, with values or goodness.

If, on the other hand, a young man whose wife may have died early in their marriage becomes a monk, it would be incorrect to maintain that he finally found his vocation. It is more accurate to declare that he had a vocation to marriage and, later, one to the monastery. One vocation is not more important or valuable than the other. They are merely different.

~~~~~~~~

God gives everyone a vocation.

Our task is to discern not *whether* we have a vocation but *which* vocation God calls us to, and how we might respond with integrity and love.

All vocations from God are sacred and all human beings who follow them have a sacred calling. God does not favor one person more than another simply because of the vocation which that person pursues. God judges us by our willingness to respond and to live out our vocation seriously and wholeheartedly.

How does one discern one's vocation?

The most immediate indication of our vocation is a sense of what makes us happy and of where our talent seems to be. The will of God for us is our happiness, and that happiness is made manifest in what we like to do and are able to do competently to enrich our own lives and the lives of others.

There is a deeper dimension to this vocation issue, however, which we have not yet addressed.

A vocation is more than the lifestyle we follow or the career choices we make. Each one of us is more than a priest or a husband, a mother or a nun. The most basic calling of all, the most sacred level of vocation, is the summons God gives us to become the person we are meant to be. This destiny involves not only ourselves but God and others as well.

It is possible, as we have seen, for the same person

3

to be husband and monk at different stages of life, or wife and single person in other contexts. The abiding reality which unites these diverse lifestyles is the vocation each of us has been given to become the person God has called us to be.

What we are suggesting is that every human being, from the very origins of his or her life, has a vocation or calling from God to be a person in a particular and unique manner.

We might go further and affirm that each person does not "have" a vocation but "is" a vocation. Each human life is a sacred calling by the very fact that it exists. We are created in the image and likeness of God — an image and a likeness that, as we shall see, calls us to be companions for one another.

~~~~~~~~~

If each of us is a vocation by our very presence in life, then each of us is creative. Creativity is the hallmark of human life. Animals and machines are not damaged if they constantly perform in an habitual manner, but human beings are.

Jesus was a creative person. The fact that the norm for his community was not law and rule but love and trust is an indication of his creativity. It was to be the Spirit, not custom, which would guide the community.

Creativity begins with the conviction that our own ideas and feelings, our emotions and insights are valuable. We often do not become aware of this or believe in it unless we are surrounded by people who listen to us and value us. This is why community is important not only to the development of creativity but also to the entire spiritual life.

Each human being is creative in a different way. No matter how much living is done by others, living has never happened before in the ways it is happening to this person. Each life is unique.

Jesus did not seek out the most impressive people of his day when he sought disciples to share and to carry on his creative vision of life. The talented and the intelligent were welcome. But, for the most part, the followers of Jesus and especially his closest companions were people society would not have considered creative. They were fishermen and laborers, the poor and the disadvantaged, the unlettered and the unnoticed. Jesus did not surround himself with people whose educations were elegant, whose professions were prestigious, whose names were renowned. The conclusion one is compelled to make is that everyone is capable of creativity if each is allowed to be creative and is encouraged when that creativity is expressed.

Every story must be heard. We ought not to allow only an elitist minority to tell their stories and force others into silence; we must not celebrate only a few and neglect the gifts of the many.

Perhaps the privileged and most effective place to generate creativity is the family. The family is the community where everyone's face and name are known, where life histories are shared, where birthdays are remembered and dreams are told, where memories are kept and absences mourned.

The very origins of a family are not conventional. Two people love without fear and trust without reserve. From this relationship the willingness to have children is born, and when they come into existence life is revealed as miraculous.

The birth of each child is filled with promise and potential, so unpredictable in its outcome and unlimited in its possibilities that it is not foolish to ask whether this child will save the world in a new way, or compose music the human ear has never heard, or create poetry the human heart will never forget. Any child might be the one to paint so brilliantly that color itself seems to be life.

Who is to say, then, that the ideas and feelings, the emotions and insights of any human being are expendable? Who is to say that children can be discounted and adults ignored? Who is to say that human history has limits and to declare what those limits are? Who is to say that human actions are circumscribed or that human beings are not relatively infinite? Who is to say that the future can be interpreted only in terms of the past?

The world is spun glory and every human being, made in such a world, is filled with radiance. Every person is embodied grace, someone for the sake of whom God has again cleared the chaos and the darkness.

Even those who resist us and reject us serve the creative enterprise. A musical instrument must be subjected to stress before music can be made. Paint must be twisted and distorted before it becomes a landscape or a human face. Words must be compelled into new relationships before there is poetry.

Creativity comes out of pain as well as joy, out of rejection as well as acceptance. The difference between suffering which destroys us and suffering which creates us is the conviction that it is all worthwhile, and the discovery of a community which assures us that our conviction is theirs.

The essence of creativity is transformation, the transubstantiation of the familiar into the priceless, of the unworthy into the sublime.

It is not money or physical resources which are most pathetically wasted in life. It is life itself.

A protest against this must be made.

The ecology most endangered today is not the air or the seas, the earth or the waters. The most endangered environment today is the human heart.

A protest against this must be made.

The most effective way to protect the planet is to protect the people in it. When people sense that they count, when they sense that their existence is valuable, they handle all that enters their lives with reverence.

Can anyone surpass the reverence a composer has for sound? Or the reverence a painter has for color? Or a poet for words? Or a mother for her child?

~~~~~~~~~

Life after death seems reasonable if one reflects on how little of the life we are given is used in this world. So much hidden music, masked color, muted words! So many dreams interrupted, journeys cancelled! So many stories never shared!

Eternity may well be the only environment which can support all the creative potential unleashed in history by each human being and, more, by all of them together. The human heart may well require the ecology of eternity for its proper nourishment.

It is, therefore, not a mere flight of fancy to suggest that every person is creative. It is sober and empirical truth; it is practical and solid thinking.

Each human person must search for the community and the relationships which honor creativity.

The dream we have dreamed from the beginning of time is that all of us might make up one family, and that all human beings might be friends. Were this to occur, we would unleash an energy and life system on this planet which the world itself could not contain. We would enlighten the darkness of the universe and, literally, reach the point where the universe expands into the void. We would do all this if we could only believe that life is not conventional.

Life, as we have said, is inexhaustible. Deep in the human heart, there are infinite sources of renewal and re-creation.

~~~~~~~~~~

The world is sacrament. It is filled with a divine presence, charged with mystery and grace at every turn. Birth gives us the senses with which to perceive this world in a fully human manner. We do not know how animals process their experience of the world, but we do know that they do not see it with human vision, or touch it with human feeling, or love it with human passion. And so birth is decisive not only for us, but also for the world.

Birth gives us sensitivities with which to perceive the world in a spiritual manner. We need to know that the glory of this world is not permanent, but that neither are its shadows. We need to know that the world is not the result of cosmic capriciousness or accident, but that it emerges with order and grace from the mighty intelligence and love of God.

We need to know that the world is not limited by its circumference, but that it is a sacrament, with endless depths of meaning and mystery. We need to know that the biology of life in this world is complemented by a theology of salvation and grace. We need to know that God sent an only-begotten Savior to us, and that the Spirit dwells in the heart of this planet. We need to know that our memories include not only the drama of life and the history of human action, but also stories about God and the biography of our Brother, Jesus, who took us into the larger community of the divine family.

We need to know that this planet is a liturgy in its own right, a worship service of God's suffering and death, a Eucharist of God's healing and resurrection. We need to know that our planet is a threshold of heaven, that its endless circles around the star which gives it life are a journey of the Magi to the birth of God. We need to know that God's mother was born here, in a town we can identify, and that the emergence of God in our world, with human senses and a body like ours, was somehow the first and last moment in the world's life.

We need to know that in the wheat fields of Galilee and Iowa, and on the tables of Jerusalem and Rome, the bread of life is made and broken. We need to know that in the vineyards of Judea and California and in the cellars of Nazareth and New York, the wine of memory is crushed and reborn. The world is a sanctuary and a supper room where mystery is enacted and encountered, where sacraments are made and received, where life is nourished and immortalized.

Let us, therefore, sing songs of courage and love.

The world is no small place to be. The planet is of no little consequence. The world is graced and so are we. Each of us influences human history and even makes a difference to the divine. Every person, therefore, has a value we can hardly exaggerate.

If all this be true, it is not excessive to declare that every person has a divine and sacred calling, and that creativity is the hallmark of human existence.

Reflection

Together... A People Set Apart

Before the Second Vatican Council, a lay person was defined as someone who participated in the apostolate of the hierarchy.

This definition implied that the hierarchy had a sacred vocation and the laity did not.

At the Second Vatican Council, the laity were defined as members of the People of God, an image used for the whole Church.

This image allows all the People of God to be seen as equal in the Church in terms of our calling and membership. It is true, of course, that some exercise different roles in the Church. This, however, does not destroy that fundamental equality which we have together as baptized Christians.

We are, together, as Christ observes, the salt of the earth and the light of the world (Mt 5:13-14). We are, together, as St. Paul writes, the Body of Christ; each member is important for all the other members (1 Cor 12:12-31). We are, together, as St. Peter notes, a chosen race, a royal priesthood, a consecrated nation, a people set apart (1 Pt 2:9-10).

Reflection

Creativity

Each of us is gifted with creativity because we are, after all, made in the image of the infinite Creator. Still our inclination is to see as creative only those who in a public way reveal to us the beauty of human life by the form and shape they give to human experience.

But we have only to look, to see that our

own daily lives are filled with creative possibilities. Consider the care we take to create peace and order in our homes, to prepare and serve a meal, to make our living or working environment an expression of who we are. Every time we take pleasure in the design and pattern of life around us—or in beauty itself—we are living creatively. Creativity is a way of seeing as well as a way of being. Every day is filled with "creative" moments; we have only to recognize them.

Chapter Two

Contemplation

In the many decades I have spent counselling people no single discovery has surprised me more than the vast number of people who have little regard for themselves. I have been astonished, not at the complacency or self-satisfaction of people, but at their sense of their own worthlessness. This is especially true when people talk about whether or not their lives are holy, and whether or not their marriages and careers are sacred.

I have concluded from this that most people are frightened about their own humanity. People tend to regard as sacred those who are far removed from the daily experiences of human life. Someone who lived in another century, or who is alive today but leads an exotic life, perhaps as an isolated missionary or hermit, is seen as holy. The further people are removed from maintaining a marriage or raising a family, from making money or making love, from paying bills or shopping for food, the holier they seem to be.

13

This is unfortunate because it eliminates almost everyone in the world from the sacred.

Every person is sacred. Every human life is a parable, a story which has spiritual value. The Spirit of God hovers over each one of us and breathes a creative Word into our hearts. This is the ground where the holy takes root. It can flourish in every human being, even in the worst of us.

The Gospel makes this point repeatedly. Jesus deals with thieves and murderers, with prostitutes and hypocrites, with prodigal sons and arrogant rulers. He turns from no one.

It is a pity that so many people have lost sight of the holiness of their lives, the sacred reality of their existence, the sacramentality of their own experience.

This book seeks the preservation and dignity of human life. It enlists the reader as a participant in that enterprise by recognizing the meaning and the irreplaceable value of the very person reading this book. If we value ourselves, we shall value others and value the world. If we value ourselves, we shall find God. For God is a possibility and a presence who becomes all the more real for us as we explore the sacredness of our life. God is the larger meaning we reach for as we perceive that the meaning of our life, of our origins and destiny, cannot be measured by the brief time we have on earth or by the limited horizon of this world.

God is the mystery we encounter as we accept the mystery of ourselves. God is the most exalted affirmation we can make about ourselves and about all of life. If life comes from God, then, it is truly a creative calling to sacred and contemplative purposes.

The word "contemplative" has the sound of something "churchy" about it. It suggests something exotic, even cloistered, removed from everyday experience and, perhaps, even from any capacity to attract us.

We suggest, however, that the word and the idea behind it are deeply human.

The etymology of the word "contemplative" suggests that every person is a temple, a church, a place where God dwells. Each human heart is a sanctuary because God has made it a home for the divine presence; each human life is a sacrament because God is revealed through it.

We can make these assertions in less theological language. Every person is filled with value. Each human heart is worthy of our knowledge and love, even of our sacrifice and care. Each human life is a mystery, dense with meaning, because it is always more wonderful than we suspect.

Human life is so rich and complex that we can hardly grasp it. It is elusive, mysterious and overwhelming. It happens so quickly and at such depth that we cannot keep up with it. It is so unpredictable and astonishing that we find it difficult to connect the present with the past, and even to discern the consequences of all this for the future. Human life is bewildering in its wholeness. The tragic moments contribute something to our life; the exuberant moments clearly do this as well.

And so, unless we reflect and meditate, unless we

stop and contemplate, unless we become receptive and quiet, we shall lose our way in our own life.

All people are propelled into contemplative moments.

Parents at a wedding of a son or daughter review their lives and reflect on the passage of time. They silently contemplate the miracle which has brought their children to such a momentous event and to such a level of possession of their own lives.

Family members at a wake or funeral meditate about the fragility of life and about the relationship they have just lost. They wonder about when death will visit them, whether they will be ready, how they will respond, what death itself means.

The mother of a newborn holds the child with reverence and faith, with love and hope, with a tenderness which is exquisite, with thoughts of her own inadequacy and of the greatness of life, astonished at the wonder which has occurred in and through her body.

A father may ask himself, as his son leaves home for career or education, for marriage or formal religious life, if he was truly the father he should have been and how he succeeded or failed in the relationship.

We are propelled into these contemplative moments by other, less significant events.

Driving alone in an automobile, we may reflect on whether we are generous enough with the people who need us. We may realize, all of a sudden, that we are not young anymore and begin to think about what that means.

In the middle of a restless night, we may doubt the value of our lives and wonder about the significance and the rightness of what we have done with them. We may question the order of our priorities and wonder whether we could have made better choices.

We may blame ourselves for losing patience as we travel alone in an airplane, or we may thank God for spouses and children as we see people greet one another with exuberance at a terminal.

A television program or a frightening rainstorm, a birthday party or an autumn walk, a near collision with another car or a winter snowfall, the Christmas season or the beginning of spring may become an occasion for life review and reflective silence.

We are suggesting that contemplative experiences abound in life and are built into the structure of our existence. They are present in the unforgettable moments of life and in our everyday activities.

Life is so rich and complex that it needs to be thought about, or else we lose its significance.

Contemplation enables us to do a number of things. It makes our complex lives simple and manageable. We begin to discern patterns and meaning rather than disorder and chaos.

Contemplation makes our lives more human, rescues us from rigid schedules, saves us from cultural obsession, peer pressure and frenzy.

Without contemplative moments, our lives become hectic and we lose our tranquility. No one wants to be in the presence of someone who is out of control, someone who has no time for us, someone who is always distracted and who leads a whirlwind

life of superficial activity. We prefer to be with someone who is peaceful and who listens to us, someone
who has gained wisdom from living and who does
not engulf us with frenetic behavior.

Contemplation, therefore, is not only available to
all of us. It is also desirable. It is not an exotic experience but a life experience and a human experience. Contemplation enables us to appreciate the
only life we have, to value the moments and people
who make up our lives, to be grateful and serene,
resilient and resourceful.

Contemplation enables us to do more with our
lives. It preserves us from wasting time and energy
on envy and vengeance, on nursing offenses and
feeding our obsessions. It enables us to be creative
rather than complex. It gives us almost two lifetimes
in one as it keeps us focused on the things which
matter most. Planning a day and keeping a schedule
do not save us as much time and energy as learning
to be more contemplative with our lives.

If we are all contemplative, to a degree, we have
already experienced its value. The point of this book
is to encourage us to expand the contemplative moments. If we know how important such moments are
for us, we may give them more attention and time as
they occur.

We might also add occasions for contemplation by
creating more opportunities for it. Some people rise
a little earlier in the morning and spend some moments alone, over coffee, perhaps, or walking, watch-
ing the sunrise or experiencing the silence.

Eventually, thoughts about life become thoughts

about God. We might support those thoughts by reading Scripture or by asking God to be our companion. We might think about the people we love and say a prayer for them. We might consider our anxieties and fears and reach for God's assistance.

All of a sudden, we find that we are praying, not just the formal prayers we learned from others but personal prayers from the heart. These prayers are prompted by the fullness of our lives and the nearness of God. Such moments are deeply human, beautifully contemplative, thoroughly Christian.

Many people are not attracted to prayer because prayer for them has been an experience which has nothing to do with their lives. Some people find prayer artificial and unreal. It is no wonder they give up on it. No one of us likes to do boring things.

What people reject is very often not prayer but a distortion of it. Real prayer has something to do with life, with our life.

It is a loss to miss the life contemplation brings.

Perhaps the chapters of this book may be a source of contemplative reading for some. If that happens, this book will have been used in the most worthy way the author could possibly imagine.

Reflection

The Prayer Of Presence

The following pattern of prayer can lead you to contemplation. The faithful practice of this mantra-like prayer will attune your inner self to awareness of the presence of God, not just in moments of prayer, but in all dimensions of life. The moment of awareness comes when you are no longer speaking, but only listening.

In God's presence you will gradually see your life and all that fills it in a new perspective, and you will be given power to respond to the inspirations the Spirit offers you.

• STEP INTO SILENCE

Obey Christ's command: "Whenever you pray, go to your room, close your door, and pray to your Father in private" (Mt 6:6).

In any place of quiet take a relaxed posture, perhaps sitting or kneeling, a position which you can maintain without movement or disturbance for fifteen minutes. Close the door of noise, anxieties, plans, anger and business behind you. Begin a slow rhythm of deep breathing. The paced inhaling and exhaling will invite you to listen to God's voice.

20

• GO BEYOND THE NOISE

During the first moments of attuning to your inner silence, quietly eliminate those distracting concerns which vie with God's nearness. One way this can be done is with the rhythmic breathing. Imagine distractions being cast away with each exhaling breath. Silence will pervade. You will become receptive to the voice of God who speaks without words.

• LISTEN TO GOD'S WORD

The regular reading of sacred Scripture will provide you with an endless supply of inspirational, prayerful pairs of words to be used as a sort of biblical chant. Select two such words or simple phrases of equal number of syllables so that the rhythm is balanced. Now repeat them in your inner voice: one word as you inhale, the other as you exhale. Let us take some examples.

From Psalm 27 you may be inspired to choose one of the following pairs as steps to contemplative prayer:

v. 1: your light — no fear.
v. 7: pity me — answer me.
v. 8: I seek — your face.
v.11: teach me — lead me.
v.13: I see — goodness.
v.14: have hope — be strong.

• SUBMISSION

As this biblical mantra becomes the background music of your consciousness, the temple of your interior silence will gradually lose its constraining walls and you will find yourself possessed by God's presence. Follow the Spirit's inspiration. Submit to the feelings that are given you. Respond to these gifts with a silent expression of joy, gratitude, praise, sorrow, love, trust... Maintain the rhythmic breathing, even though the biblical chant you have been repeating may have given way to complete silence. If distracting thoughts disturb this peace, just take up the chant again.

When this audience with your Creator has come to an end, allow yourself some moments before turning to the business of the day. Reflect upon the inspirations you have received. Savor the power you have experienced. Exercise it with gratitude during the coming hours.

Chapter Three

Love

To love is to give life its most human expression. No human institution is more persistently and creatively on the side of life than marriage. Marriage probably offers the greatest potential for human happiness to the vast majority of human beings. Married or not, however, every person has the potential to be life-giving.

This life force is manifest just as strongly, sometimes more creatively, in people who choose not to marry or who do not conceive children of their own. It is present in the considerable number of years we live, in youth and maturity, without marriage partners. It is operative in the decades of life people live after their children are grown and independent.

The human animal, so to speak, is a life-giver in so many creative ways that we find it difficult to catalogue them. As far as we can determine, animal life as such seldom entails lifelong friendship, lifelong mating partnerships, lifelong parental sensitivities. All of these are the norm in human life.

Human beings seek not only to be life-givers but to give life for as long as they live, to people for whom they feel responsible.

Life-giving, on the human level, is far more than biological or organic life. Indeed, we might even affirm that the genetic transmission of life is the least impressive of those elements which humanize us. It is the love which accompanies and precedes this transmission but, more, the love which follows forever after which is the hallmark of human life.

God has given us the great privilege to be life-givers. We give this life with diversity and variety in more instances than we can number or catalogue. God also gives life in an incredible multiplicity of ways. The physical forms of life on this planet are one example of how abundantly and exuberantly God gives life. Human beings are limited in the physical forms of life they can create, but they seem limitless in the cultural and spiritual life they can generate around them.

There is something relatively infinite about the human capacity for love, about the life-giving potential of people.

We are those who dream of life beyond death, in a realm of happiness and immortality where all life is honored and no life is injured. We are those who believe that life has its origins in nothing less than God. God is the word we use to designate a Presence so filled with life that it is impervious to death, so graced with wisdom that it can care for all life that was or is or will be. God is the word we use for Love that is infinite.

We are convinced, with an optimism which exceeds imagination and a confidence with borders on boldness, that we are co-creators with God for the life of the world. We have been invited to this by a God who has made our bodies instruments for the transmission of life, and who has made our hearts restless until they give life emotionally and spiritually. It is an awesome and an endless task, a grave and lighthearted responsibility, a solemn and joyful summons.

God brings into existence male and female and gives them to each other for life. In the first chapter of Genesis, their creation is equal and simultaneous, and both are fashioned in the image and likeness of God.

The new human beings, made like God, are to act like God who, in creating all things, found them good and loved them. As co-creators with God, they are, then, summoned from the beginning to a life liturgy. They are to be its priests, its celebrants, guardians of life and consecrators of it, in love.

They are to give the world images of God and images of themselves, by obeying all that God has taught them.

When God thinks about human life, in Genesis, the first thought in God's mind is not prayer or Church, formal liturgy or ritual sacraments, prohibitions or penalties, rules or laws. The first thought in God's mind is that human beings are to be love-makers and life-givers. The first couple, like all men and women after them, are to be priests who bring the world God through the creation and sacramentality of human life in a liturgy of love. From the moment of creation, human beings are wedded to life and to each other. This commitment is so binding that God does not break it after the Fall. Adam and Eve are allowed to leave Eden, with their privilege of making life and love intact. All else, save this, is left behind in Paradise.

We are invited by God to bring life into existence everywhere and with everyone. We are to generate life biologically sometimes, but to create life spiritually always.

Like God, we are wedded to life and the fruit of this marriage is the life of the world.

The fact that love is the greatest of our doings is not always evident to us as we go about our daily tasks. Most people, however, given a moment's reflection, know that love is the best of them.

Everything tells us that we have been made for love. Our bodies and hearts are defined by love and shaped by it. Our finest artistic achievements, our best poetry and most exhilarating dance, our finest paintings and most memorable music, our unforgettable stories and most impressive experiences are those of love.

Love never leaves us barren. A life of love begets love in those around us. Each of us is needed as a resource of love for the world. Every time love finds expression in us it makes it possible for others to believe in love as a priority in their lives.

We preach the Gospel best, not by words but with our hearts. We are the Church most effectively not in receiving sacraments but in giving love.

The wonder of love lies in our growing into all that love demands: a willingness to give of ourselves, to be open to the need of the other, and, even to risk our life if need be. "There is no greater love than this: to lay down one's life for one's friend."

Like so much in life that is meaningful, love has a terrible beauty.

Love does make demands: on the one who loves and on the one who is loved. Love is not always easy, but it is in every way life-giving.

> Love is patient; love is kind. Love is not jealous, it does not put on airs, it is not snobbish. Love is never rude, it is not self-seeking, it is not prone to anger; neither does it brood over injuries.... There is no limit to love's forbearance, to its trust, its hope, its power to endure. (1 Cor 13:4, 5, 7)

Reflection

Love Till the End

Judas caught Jesus' attention among his many followers. Later he became one of Jesus' closest friends, one of the trusted twelve whom Jesus personally selected and sent "to preach the good news and expel demons" (Mk 3:13-15). Some say Jesus chose him out of the ranks of the revolutionary Zealots bent on driving out the Roman occupational army, by force if necessary.

Judas knew how to carry things through and to get things done. Jesus put him in charge of the common purse. Judas had a sense for the little people, the landless, unemployed and exploited whose cause he championed. He was glad when he could share something with them. Maybe that is what Jesus liked most about him: Judas combined courage, conviction and concern.

What went wrong? And what does this tragic shattering of human affection tell us about Jesus' love for others?

Judas was becoming disillusioned. "Love your enemies" (Mt 5:44)? "Forgive seventy-seven times" (Mt 18:22)? How far will this Jesus go? The conflict of interests was mounting. Then the "extravagant waste" of precious ointment tipped the scale. Almost a year's worth of wages! Judas became indignant.

While Jesus was in Bethany at the house of Simon the Leper, a woman carrying a jar of costly perfume came up to him at table and began to pour it on his head. The disciples grew indignant, protesting: "What is the point of such extravagance? This could have been sold for a good price and the money given to the poor." Jesus said to them: "Why do you criticize the woman? By pouring this perfume on my body, she has contributed toward my burial preparation." (Mt 26:6-13)

That was it! Judas wanted nothing to do with a loser.

He went off to the chief priests and said, "What will you give me if I hand him over to you?" They paid him thirty pieces of silver, and from that time on he kept looking for an opportunity to hand him over. (Mt 26:14-16)

Judas had become resolute, hardened. He traded Jesus for the price of a slave. Was it ambition, greed, or had he gone back to his first agenda—freedom by the sword? Whatever it was, Jesus' love pursued him, protected him, invited him. He never excluded Judas, but neither did he seek Judas' love at any price. He always confronted Judas with the truth, and with an alternative: power is for service; life is for love. But Judas must choose this freely for himself.

They were at supper, and the devil had already put it into the mind of Judas to betray him. Then Jesus poured water into a basin and began to wash the disciples' feet. "You are clean, though not all of you." He knew who was going to betray him.

"Do you understand what I have done to you?" Jesus said to them. "If I, your Lord and Master have washed your feet, you must wash each other's feet."

Then Jesus became deeply disturbed.

"One of you is going to betray me." He dipped a piece of bread into the dish and gave it to Judas. "What you are going to do, do quickly." None of the others at table understood why he had said this. They thought Jesus was telling him to give something to the poor. Judas took the bread and went out. It was night. (Jn 13)

There was no scene. No "After all I've done for you." No belittling. Not even later in the garden when the guards came with swords and clubs to arrest Jesus. Judas went up to him, "Greetings, Rabbi," and kissed him. Jesus said to him, "My friend, do you betray me with a kiss?"... Jesus loved Judas till the end.

Chapter Four

Sacrament

There are many angles from which we can evaluate the notion of sacrament. In the strictest sense, sacraments are ritual events, profound expressions of Church life, symbols through which an encounter with Christ is realized. In the larger sense, sacraments are physical and concrete phenomena which bring an awareness of the presence of God and the mystery of life to us.

It is in this larger meaning that we wish to consider the idea of sacramentality. On this level, the word is sacramental. The beauty of the world, and its capacity to generate and sustain life, mediate God to us and fill us with a sense of awe. One can ponder the world and, all of a sudden, become involved with the reality of God. As we encounter the world, we find that we meet not only the physical structure of the planet but intimations of divinity and immortality. We find the divine in this world because God has chosen to link revelation with physical events.

This means of revelation is startling and consoling. God is transcendent, beyond us, apparently un-approachable, invisible, almighty, inconceivable, awesome, bewildering, infinite. God exceeds all our categories of thinking, imagination and language.

And yet, God is present in a leaf or a flower, in the birth of an animal and the embrace of a child, in human love and at every stage of life. The God of the universe is also the God of each moment of its life, a God who penetrates all the specifics of reality. Be-cause this is so, everything is sacramental in the larger sense of the word. There is a holiness and sanctity deep down in everything. Nothing is totally secular; everything is radically sacred, sanctified in its very roots.

The notion of a sacramental universe is central to Catholic and contemporary spirituality. Sacramen-tality reminds us that everything and everyone is to be dealt with reverently.

As far as we can determine, the created order finds its most profound and mysterious expression in human life. The sacramentality of the world seeks to create a sacrament which expresses the world and exceeds it at one and the same moment. It ac-complishes this in human beings.

A human life is circumscribed and defined by the world, limited by it and enclosed within it. And yet, human life is always beyond the very reality which embraces it. Human beings, for example, can im-agine life on another planet or an existence beyond death, which the world cannot encompass. Human beings can believe in a divine reality which eludes the physical senses and surpasses the created order.

In this, human beings are like God, sacramentalized in a world and somehow able to exist beyond it.

It would be tragic if we saw our lives only as pragmatic enterprises. For many people, life is little more than an agenda of practicalities. It is a series of tasks, of projects and plans.

There is something depressing about this reduction of life to manageable goals and efficient objectives. The end result of this prodigious effort is a reality considerably less in value than the people who have expended their lives on it. To trade a life, for example, for financial security and corporate promotions and nothing more is to waste a life.

We do not intend to suggest that financial security or corporate promotions have no value. People require money to live; recognition of our work is a human need. It is the misplacement of these as the full and final purposes of life which is unfortunate.

Some people claim that they are not principally motivated by money and advancement, but their behavior with their family and friends shows that they do not believe what they say. The sacrifice of profound human experiences for income and job titles leads to a dreary life.

No salary is worth a marriage. No income bracket is large enough to compensate a child for years of companionship lost to a busy parent. No respect given to us because of our affluence or power can measure up to the respect people give us for the worth of our presence.

Affluence does not bring us what it promises.

With great wealth comes the fear of losing it, the narrow focus of managing and increasing it, the suspicion that others, even family, cannot be trusted.

Nor does corporate advancement deliver the security we assume. No level of power releases us from accountability to others or makes us immune to losing it. No level of success protects our vanity from injury. The more prominent we become the more criticism we receive. The larger the scope a job encompasses the more likely it is that our shortcomings and fallibilities will be made manifest.

We are not presenting these ideas to discourage people in their search for financial adequacy and career satisfaction. We are merely calling attention to myths and distortions about these objectives which our culture often promotes.

Money and career cannot bring us tranquility. They bring us attention from others and absorption in themselves. It is human relationship in a sacramental world which brings us peace.

~~~~~~~~~

One of the most damaging choices young people can make is the choice of a career only because it offers money and power. There is a great deal of pressure on young people to do this, pressure from parents and peers and counselors.

Any career has, in itself, the capacity to bring us human worth and happiness. None of them can do this, however, if the reasons for our choice are exclusively income and advancement. It is sad to see young, idealistic people sacrifice the choices they know would have made them happy. They sometimes do this because they have been frightened into believing that money and power are the essence of life.

Each one of us is a priest and a sacrament, not in a tedious "churchy" or institutional sense but in the sense that consecration and commitment, fidelity and community, love and life belong to all the stages of our existence.

God is at issue in us.

We do not belong to an income bracket or a corporation. We belong to ourselves and our families, to our friends and communities, to the whole human race and to God.

We do not belong to an employer. We belong to this world and the paradise beyond it. We are not defined by our financial resources and by our level in the company hierarchy. We elude all definitions and we eclipse all categories.

We are made for infinite possibilities and divine promises, for a future which has no end to it and a life that is immortal. We have been made for nothing less than God.

Reflection

Taking Time

I have never been able to forget a relatively young man whom I met one day at a meeting. He had been unemployed for a while. It seemed unlikely he would find a job in the immediate future.

I might add that this meeting took place in another country where job prospects were not promising. As a result of this, the man in question was living in financial stress even though he was a person of remarkable intelligence and talent. He was one of those people we meet and always remember.

In any case, I asked him how he coped with his situation. He told me that one of the things he did was to take long walks every day with his young son. Sometimes they would fish together; other times they would try to build something as a team. "We have come to know each other well," he added. "I, of course, love him very much."

I was deeply moved by the conversation. I thought of the enduring memory the son would have of his father and of how few sons have such an opportunity. I reflected on the fact that the son of this man was one of the luckiest people in the world. No amount of money could convince the son of his worth more thoroughly than the time father and son had with each other. They built together not only things but an indestructible bond and an imperishable love. How lucky they were!

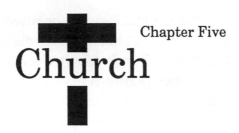

Chapter Five

Church

There arc, of course, many ways to define the Church. The definition most Catholics assume to be the only correct one sees the Church as a large, international organization with Pope, cardinals, bishops and priests as the real Church and the laity as a marginal appendage to this structure. In such a view one is not at peace with the Church unless one has the approval of the Church's ranking officers. It is true that God is more than the Church but, for most Catholics, acceptance by God is tied into acceptance by the official Church.

This definition of the Church is widespread partly because there are some elements of truth in it. The Church is, indeed, a large, international structure, the largest in the world. And this massive structure is not incidental to the Church's life. It is important and impressive.

We might also affirm that the official Church represents, in its teaching and life, elements which are crucial to Christ's message. In a number of instances, therefore, the official Church position is close to what God might require of us. An example may help.

The official Church teaches that the bombing of innocent civilian populations in war is always morally evil. It would be difficult to imagine that Christ would not have taught the same message were Christ still historically alive.

The official Church teaches, furthermore, that human beings are not to be rejected because they are physically maimed, mentally deficient, racially different, religiously diverse. One hears in such instruction the echo and resonance of Christ's voice.

There are, however, aspects of the definition which began this chapter which are not as correct as they ought to be. The Church, for example, lives more by its spirit and tradition than it does by its structure. A comparison may help here.

Human life is sustained and valued primarily by the spirit of the person. The body is indispensable, but the spirit seems to shape and form the contours of our life more definitively.

A Catholic might be described effectively as someone who embodies the spirit of Christ and of the Church rather than as someone who is legally part of the organization. One element need not militate against the other, but there are priorities. In the best of possibilities, these two realities complement each other. In actual fact, there might be divergences. When this occurs, the Church is found primarily in its spirit.

It is also invalid to assume that a lay person is a less vital part of the Church's life than clerical officers are. One can understand why this assumption is made. If people suppose structure means more than spirit, they will conclude that ranking in the organization makes one more Catholic than those who have a lesser legal and canonical role to play.

The Church, indeed, does not teach that the laity are less vital to the Church than the clergy. Nonetheless, the official Church on occasion, and lay Catholics more often, behave as though the laity were incidental to the Church's life. Few things are more at variance with Christ's teaching.

Jesus, in terms of the Jewish religious establishment of his day and its officers, was a lay person. He was not a Jewish priest nor was he a candidate for special Temple and liturgical service as a Levite.

Jesus insisted that love rather than ritual or rank was the hallmark of a disciple. Love, of course, knows no boundaries and fosters no divisions, even institutional ones.

If we are going to create a contemporary Catholic spirituality, our attitude toward the Church and our definition of it are extremely important. One way to look at this question is to try to discern what it meant to be a disciple of Christ in the beginning and to define our role in the Church in reference to this. This is not to maintain that other, later developments in the Church's life are not also urgent and important. But there are priorities.

The very term "disciple of Christ" is less familiar to many Catholics as a description of their identity. It may even have a Protestant ring to it for some. It is easier for most Catholics, perhaps, to view themselves as members of the Church, as Catholics, rather than as disciples of Christ.

There are, once again, valid reasons why people think of themselves in this way. In the best of our possibilities, a disciple of Christ and a Catholic are the same thing. But for many Catholics, "disciple of Christ" sounds vague and "Catholic" gives a concrete idea of what a disciple is and how a disciple ought to behave. There is further support for preferring "Catholic" to "disciple". "Catholic" already implies a community or organization to which believers belong. This seems less isolated and lonely than the term "disciple".

Granted all this, it is instructive to look at the term "disciple" so that we might understand better our role as Catholics in the Church.

~~~~~~~~

A "disciple of Christ" is someone who is convinced that in the life and teaching of Jesus it is possible to find the will and love of God. Jesus is, therefore, the normative experience for encountering God. And so, a disciple remembers Jesus and celebrates him. A disciple is deeply moved by the Gospel and profoundly challenged by it.

A disciple is someone who comes into the company and the community of Jesus with no desire for rank or prestige, someone who wishes to exercise no authority but rather to be obedient to the spirit and memory of Jesus. A disciple presents his or her sins to Jesus for forgiveness, his or her hopes to Christ for fulfillment.

Christianity is fundamentally a relationship between disciple and Lord, between believer and Christ, between friend and Savior. It is only later that questions of structure and clarity of teaching, moral norms and legal prescriptions are added. These later "additions" are neither unworthy nor unnecessary nor unhelpful. As we apply discipleship to all the varied aspects of daily life, we run into confusion and conflict. We seek guidance and assistance from one another and, eventually, a structure is put in place.

It is essential for our sense of contemporary spirituality that we learn how to hold on to the notion of being a Catholic while we emphasize the centrality of our discipleship.

The Church cannot always solve dilemmas in our life, nor challenge us in the specific ways we need to be challenged. If we have a sense that we are disciples, more of our daily insecurities will be addressed and more will be demanded of us. As more is asked of us, more will be given.

Discipleship emphasizes the individual relationship with Christ and the love which sustains it. "Catholic" emphasizes the communal nature of that relationship and the commitment which supports it. The terms are not mutually exclusive. Indeed, they complement and develop each other.

If there is any human being in history who has the capacity of being considered a "universal person" for all ages and cultures, it may well be Christ. This is not to deny that Buddha or Mohammed were people of enormous holiness and impressive character. But even Buddhists or Muslims do not put Buddha or Mohammed at the center of their religious system as Christians do with Christ.

Buddhists and Muslims find Christ a compelling person even if they are not always favorable to Christianity. The Jewish community also can find in Christ someone who expresses values which are essential both for human life as such and for the Jewish tradition as well. It is not Christ but subsequent Jewish and Christian history which complicates Jewish-Christian relationships.

Jesus, perhaps, embodies the strongest expressions of forgiveness in human history. One need only consider the prayer of forgiveness for his executioners, uttered by Jesus as he is nailed to the cross. One has only to recall the wholehearted and affectionate forgiveness of the son by the father in the parable of the Prodigal Son.

Jesus, we might say, teaches the centrality of love as the essence of his religious system. We are to be known as disciples, he tells us, by our love for one another.

Jesus calls his disciples not servants but friends as he washes their feet.

Jesus intends universality in the application of his message more consciously than any other person in history. Even enemies are to be loved. Jesus gives us the parable of the Good Samaritan and assigns priority to sinners and outcasts. Jesus is always reaching beyond barriers and boundaries to rescue people with love.

Jesus describes the judgment at the end of the world as one which has as its norm not whether we were Catholic or Christian but whether we were responsible when we saw one another thirsty and hungry, lonely and sick, imprisoned and unwelcome.

The fact that these values Jesus affirms are present not only in his teaching but even in his life gives them a dramatic and sacramental quality which is simply overwhelming.

Forgiveness and the crucified Jesus; love and the Master who washes the feet of others; universality in the parables which stress the spirit rather than the law are icons and images that endure in the mind and in the emotions.

There is no person of good will who does not learn from Christ. The same may also be true of Buddha or Mohammed but our focus here is on the application of the terms Christian and Church to the whole world.

We are, furthermore, suggesting that the centrality of the very person of Christ in the Christian scheme of things and in the Gospel presentation of him, a centrality not present with other religious leaders in their system, makes it likely that Jesus may have as much claim as anyone to being the universal person in history.

In any case, all the world learns from Jesus even if everyone might not wish to be Christian or even religious. Perhaps Jesus is the very one whose life and teaching lead us to a profound encounter with other religious systems. Jesus told us there was much he had yet to teach us which he had not expressed in his own life. A disciple of Christ knows that Christ has much more to teach all of us than we have learned thus far. A disciple is, indeed "someone who learns."

Reflection

Jesus, Center of History

We might reflect further on the theme of Christ as the central person in human history.

Clearly, there has been no single person who has received more devotion from others than Christ. Buddhists and Muslims celebrate Buddha and Mohammed but put their ultimate devotion in a reality or God beyond these historical persons. Jews venerate Abraham and Moses but insist that these men are not God.

Christianity, however, claims that Jesus is not only human but also the Son of God. And so, worship of God and devotion to Christ are intertwined. No other religious system does this quite so boldly.

There is no other religious system which insists so strongly on linking the validity of a founder's teaching with the teacher's life. All that Jesus proclaims must be verified in his "biography" for the Christian system to work. And so, Christians claim that Jesus is actually sinless and that the themes of

44

his parables are reflected in his life history.

It is not only the rightness of the teaching about forgiveness of enemies which matters, but the very practice of it in the life of Jesus. No other religious system makes so much of the birth and death of its founder as Christianity does.

For these and other reasons, Christ emerges as the person in the world who seems to have played the most centralized universal role in history.

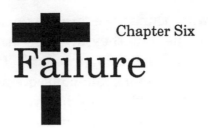

Chapter Six

Failure

We have explored an array of positive and supportive themes in the development of this book. We have seen how each person has a vocation from God, how each person is creative and contemplative, life-giving and love, sacrament and Church.

No one knows all the reasons why some people view life as a discouraging experience. This attitude is not solely the result of obstacles and misfortunes. Some people who seem to have everything, so to speak, are depressed; others who appear to have been ill-used by life are not unhappy.

There is something opaque and intractable about the mystery of evil and about our own preference at times for negativity and self-damaging choices. We astonish ourselves in life, not only by our own generosity and forgiveness of others, but also by our pettiness and vindictiveness. We all have a record of actions and tendencies which shame us as we recall them and which we know are not worthy of us or fair to others. Each of our biographies or life stories is filled with things we are anxious for people to know about us, but they are also strewn with facts we would rather have suppressed.

One of the remarkable consequences of virtue or goodness is the endless joy it gives us, even if it has led us to sacrifice some advantage or opportunity we might have had. A noble moment in our lives enlightens the rest of our lives and the lives of others. Children or friends, parents or spouses endlessly repeat, with satisfaction and respect, the heroism of a particular selfless action of ours.

On the other hand, an ignoble moment in our lives darkens our lives and diminishes the lives of others. Family and associates may become silent in shame as the deed is recalled. Excuses may be made or accusations registered. All are uncomfortable and try to hide the evil or explain it away, to balance it off with some memory of goodness, to hope that others, as they learn of it, will not think the deed was approved or that it ought to be repeated. There is endless regret about some of the unworthy things each of us has done.

~~~~~~~~

There are two unfortunate ways in which we can react to our failures. One of these is to become complacent with our failures, to settle into a level of meanness, for example, or anger, declaring that we have no other options and that people must accept us as we are.

Another unfortunate reaction to failure is to

become so fixated on failure that we do not let it go. We need to forgive ourselves even when others do not. Life is a long and complicated process; it is impossible to get it all right. The experience of failure is the price we pay for living and for being human.

The tradition of the Church, in this regard, has been sound. The Church is not complacent with failure nor fixated on it. We are reminded of our sins even as we are forgiven. Amendment is expected even though it is not always likely. Pardon requires that we name our sins and indict ourselves for them, even as we are assured that God withholds forgiveness from no one and that we must not dwell on our mistakes.

On the deepest levels of the Church's life, festivity and celebration are highly regarded and encouraged. Sin seems to have a harder time of it, so to speak, in the face of humor and in the context of joy. There is something grim and singleminded about sin, something narrow and pinched, something loveless and lifeless, something rigid and unrelieved. Humor dispels the environment in which sin grows and brings light into the shadows of our lives. Jesus observes that evil deeds are always best done in the darkness.

And so, even though failure at times is inevitable, we must go on celebrating. We celebrate, not the failure as such but the fragility of our human condition which is not perfect and yet which is not destroyed by failure, no matter how evil that failure is.

We must even, in a sense, celebrate the failure, because it has not been as dark as it once seemed to be or as it might have been. The failure teaches us something. It teaches us about our needs for others and about our dependence on God. Failure opens the way to compassion. If we never stumbled along the way, we might walk by all those who have. We minister effectively to others when we, too, know what it is like to have been wounded.

~~~~~~~~~

St. Augustine once reminded us that there could be a "happy fault." St. Paul had observed before him that sin leads to even more grace from God.

A fault is happy when it brings a level of love and healing of gratitude and peace which we never knew existed. This does not mean that we become complacent about the fault. The fault, of its very nature, has caused pain and suffering. It has harmed others and ourselves as well. It may have damaged someone in a way which makes full recovery impossible. But the fault often teaches us how marvelous life is in its capacity to recover and renew itself. Life can affirm itself and even bring light as it is being assaulted. Certainly Jesus did this as he was nailed to the cross.

The love and forgiveness which follow upon our evil choices teach us about the greatness of the human heart and the magnitude of the human spirit.

Love is not complete, for us, until it takes account of failure and embraces it. The love of ourselves is insufficient until we experience imperfection and recognize it as ours, not in complacency but in resolution and peace. Evil can never control us unless we choose to let it.

Our love of others may be inadequate until they fail in some significant manner and we assure them that they are worth more than all the damage they have done. In this way, we were all once loved from the cross.

Love is weak and unstable, superficial and, perhaps, self-serving until it reveals itself as stronger than evil and unconquered by sin, as mightier than all the forces hurled against it. In this way, we are all once loved on Easter morning.

> Love is complete when one human being says
> to another:
> You have wounded me and disappointed me.
> You have hurt me beyond description.
> But I forgive you with all my heart
> because I believe you will heal me also
> and I refuse to lose faith in you.
> I too have not been blameless.
> We need to forgive each other.

~~~~~~~~

Transformation is one of the remarkable features of biological and spiritual life. Biologically, food is transformed into the body and sustenance of an organism. Food becomes something it was not before, through a process which remains remarkable and astonishing even when we know how it occurs.

Spiritually, we are able to transform experiences into levels of reality they did not previously possess. In this sense, evil can be made to foster our spiritual life and even to strengthen the communities to which we belong.

Evil, in itself, is not a very creative reality. It is what it is and it does what it does with little variation or diversity. Evil is an imprisoning experience; confinement and incarceration enlist little creativity and less freedom.

A person who has grown in the spiritual life is, of course, wounded by the choice he or she has made for evil, or by the evil which is unleashed by another. But the evil may be transformed by such a person into an experience whose net result is an enrichment rather than a loss of life. The evil may be compensated for by deeper humility, more compassion, greater reliance on God and others, sharper insights into the nature of the self and the power of evil. As we deal with evil from others, we may reveal to them the strength of goodness and love, which is not overcome but indeed prevails. The fact that we take the evil in and do not respond with more evil manifests to others the limits of evil and the limitless character of forgiveness.

Each of us fails in life, but the responses to that failure are numberless; the creativity of overcoming that failure is inexhaustible.

~~~~~~~~~

There is a deep admiration in the human family for creative responses to evil. Newspapers and the media attest to the fascination with and the horror of evil which seizes people's attention. Crimes and tragedies would not be described in such detail and with such prominence unless people wished to be so informed. When these grim circumstances are detailed, people read or listen attentively for a time but lose interest quickly and recall such incidents with difficulty a year later.

When, however, the negative experience is accompanied by a story of heroism and virtue, people remember that redeeming characteristic more tenaciously.

Heroism in the face of evil is impressive and creates indelible memories. Fire fighters risk their lives for people they do not know and even for people against whom they have prejudice in normal circumstances. In a moment of crisis, such heroes sense only the common humanity which links us together and the horror of dying alone and in flames.

Although war is the most wrenching of all human experiences, it has led to impressive self-sacrifice for friends, for the innocent and sometimes even for the enemy.

There are other examples. People give food, when they are starving, to their children and, history records, to strangers. Others have voluntarily drowned at sea so that someone else may have a place in a lifeboat. Still others have performed impressive acts of kindness in more normal circumstances, and refused to be compensated for them or even publicly recognized.

The history of the human family is marked, unfortunately, with the reverse of this: failure and crime, tragedy and sin, exploitation and manipulation, accidents and cruelty, thoughtlessness and irresponsibility. In a sense, such occurrences are relatively easy to understand. Self-interest and envy, vengeance and incompetence, anger and vanity are comprehensible.

The astonishing fact is not that people answer evil with evil, but that they often resound with mercy and become self-giving in the face of tragedy.

We Christians should appreciate such a response more, perhaps, than anyone else. Jesus told us stories of those, such as the Good Samaritan, who overcome cruelty and indifference with love and compassion. When we hear the story of the Good Samaritan, we do not focus our attention on the robbers or on the indifferent religious officials, but on a good and gentle man who brought healing to a wounded neighbor and made evil insignificant by his goodness.

The parable takes on added significance when the storyteller himself, Jesus, is later robbed and beaten and nailed to a cross. He too was stripped of his clothes and left to die. He becomes, on the cross, not only the victim but also the Good Samaritan who, although an outcast, refuses to hate or to reject his persecutors.

When the story of Jesus is retold, we have little interest in who the executioners were, or who it was who testified against him, or who passed the sentence of death. The world has been transfixed, instead, with the character and the identity of the Crucified.

Had Jesus died with anger and denunciations against his tormentors, that would have been comprehensible. The response of Jesus, however, was creative, self-forgetful, forgiving. It was so full of human decency and love, so clear an example of divine compassion and mercy that we have been fascinated by it ever since it happened. It is impossible to know how many people have led better lives because of that one, great act of love.

~~~~~~~~~

We do not live very long without encountering negative and evil experiences. Human history reveals that such experiences are more transitory than we suspect. The memory of the human family is replete with stories of uncommon and extraordinary goodness. The stories make us want to do likewise even as we hear them.

The stories of failure and crime do not make us want to repeat them but to reverse them. The stories of recovery and goodness, of love and generosity fill us with admiration, make us wish such stories might be told of us and lead us to imitate such behavior.

Sometimes we, too, become the object of a story people tell about us, a story which may enable them to manage their own lives with dignity and courage. When this occurs, all the mistakes of our own life seem to be overcome by the very fact that we have enabled others to compensate for their failures.

Reflection

Goodness from Tragedy

The story of the Good Samaritan is familiar. We know of the beaten man and the indifferent religious officials who refused to help. We know that the beaten man was most likely, a Jew and that the one who stopped to assist him was a Samaritan. Jews and Samaritans were taught to hate each other.

There are two aspects of the story which we might underscore.

The first of these is the extent of kindness done by the Samaritan. It was dangerous and life-threatening to stop on the open road in ancient times. A crime had already been committed at this very spot. The Samaritan risks his life and gives his time to help a stranger. It took a long while to care for the man and bandage him, to take him to the inn and to stay overnight with him. The Samaritan also paid money not only for one day's lodging and care, but for all the days the beaten man needed to remain there until he recovered. The Samaritan, furthermore, must have had his own important business to perform. One did not travel for frivolous reasons in the ancient world.

A second aspect of the story concerns the reaction of the Jewish man as he recovers. He must have been astonished as he heard that he was brought to the inn by a stranger and, indeed, a Samaritan. He would never again be able to hate Samaritans or to teach his children to do so. He is, therefore, spiritually healed as he is physically restored.

Had this crime not occurred, the Jewish man might have lived his whole life hating Samaritans and teaching others to do likewise. The tragedy, which no one wishes to make light of, created more goodness in the world than its absence might have. Where there was sin, grace abounded all the more.

Chapter 7

Recovery

It is not all that remarkable that we fail. We are limited organisms, vulnerable in our every part, hurled into a world imbued with forces which generate life and undermine it all at once. The world is an awesome and dangerous place to live in.

There are endless hazards. We are expected to do a great number of things as human beings, to learn extraordinarily complex skills, to become participants in intricate and demanding communities.

A substantial percentage of our lives is expended preparing for the work we do. It is not unusual for young people to extend formal education into their second and third decade of life. One half or one third of our lives may be given to acquiring the expertise to pursue our careers.

There are other expectations. Marriage and family life are a source of almost infinite meaning and fulfillment, but they compel us to weave together the disparate threads of other lives at the most intense level of engagement imaginable.

We need to be nourished, as human beings, not only physically but emotionally, not only socially but spiritually, not only individually but corporately. There are financial and legal, linguistic and accounting, consumer and mechanical tasks to perform. The list could be continued indefinitely.

The wonder is not that we fail. The wonder is that it happens as seldom as it does and in as few instances of our lives as it does. The process of our conception, gestation and birth, in and of itself, is so complicated and hazardous that no human being can comprehend its intricacy or appreciate the dynamisms which lead it to a safe conclusion. The rapidity with which people learn to function in so many areas simultaneously is breathtaking. Mathematics and music, language and history, religious systems and cultural imperatives form an array of demands which people learn to perform without knowing how they do it.

And so, there is every reason for us to be compassionate with ourselves or others when a failure occurs.

One of the impressive achievements of the human family is the vast network for recovery it has set in place. We should not take this for granted. If someone were to evaluate the spiritual resources of human life, it would be necessary to include all the efforts which were made to assist those who falter and fail.

Jesus once told us that the final judgment would be premised on our capacity to support the lonely and the lost, the hungry and the homeless, the indigent and the injured. If we look at the structures of society and Church, of family and nation, we can affirm that the demands of Jesus have not gone wholly unheard.

As we observed earlier, human failures receive a great deal of attention. We are made conscious of how many people starve in the world each day, of where wars are being fought, of the large numbers of homeless and ill people who are neglected.

This record of our failures is heartbreaking and inexcusable. It is crucial that we remind ourselves of the suffering which goes on in the world every day if we are to keep alive our humanity and become a compassionate people.

~~~~~~~~~

Granted this, I would like us to consider elements in this equation which are not often calculated. I do not wish, in the least, to make us blind to the misery or insensitive to the pain we needlessly create in our world. There are, indeed, justifying reasons for almost endless shame, guilt and grief. To see only one child die of hunger is an assault on our senses and psyche.

But there are other things to notice.

An effort is made daily on this planet to feed five billion people and to find room for more. There is no way to measure how much love is expressed each and every day in human history: love for newborn life and for children, for spouses and parents, for friends and even former enemies, for the earth and the seas, for animals and plants, for stars and the heavens. Each day five billion people find love and offer love in such a variety of circumstances and with so many different individuals that no calculation can be made. Even the unworthy are loved.

Every day forgiveness is multiplied in all the communities where people live, and every day God is praised in prayers that never cease, from the rising of the sun to the going down of the moon. No one can make a record of how often courage is affirmed, or of how frequently people achieve victories over themselves and extend generosity to others.

Every day, all the systems for healing in our world are put into operation. Every day, injuries, from a child's bruise to an adult's terminal illness, are dealt with in compassion and tenderness. Every day mothers spend sleepless nights with frightened children and spouses keep their partners company as they die. Every day hands of love and words of comfort are brought to bear on those whose pain has become our own. Every day people share with their suffering loved ones the dreams and memories of their common journey.

Every day marriages are made and lifetime fidelities sworn. Every day homes are built and places for prayer are constructed. Every day schools are established and hospitals are put in place. Every day clothes are made and bread is broken. Every day the world is filled with birthday celebrations and worship services, decorated with candles and cakes, with balloons and streamers, with color and costumes, with lights and gifts.

Every day music is created in the world and words are put on paper. Every day landscapes are painted and people learn to dance. Every day letters seeking love and forgiveness are written and confessions of guilt formulated. Every day flowers are gathered and journeys are made to those who need us.

Every day five billion people are given another day of life. Every day a new family is begun and someone learns to walk. Every day someone utters a first word to the joy of those who hear it.

By what right do we neglect all of this? We dare not dismiss all the effort and energy, all the love and devotion which make this happen in our world, not on one day but every day. In the distant reaches of the universe and in the minute corners of our lives, God must know, as all this happens, that creation has not been in vain and that human beings have indeed honored the image in which they were made.

The spiritual life is built on themes of appreciation and gratitude. We must not allow ourselves to make little of the great things people do.

When we falter, we must know that there are numberless people ready to assist. We must not become cynical about this, disbelieving that people do care, or become vain about it, refusing to admit that we need people or assuming that no one has problems such as ours.

The Church also has impressive resources to enable people to recover.

The Gospel itself is a reminder that God and Christ do not abandon us when we sin or mess up our lives. They seek us out, as a shepherd does a lost sheep, as a father does a wayward son, as a healer does an injured person.

Jesus himself is described as having been lonely and frightened, discouraged and ignored, injured and rejected. He asks, in a sad moment, if there will be any faith on earth if he should return to it. Nor did he always prefer the way his life was going. He prays in Gethsemane for another outcome if that is possible.

The Gospel is a story of ultimate victory, but it is not an easy victory, nor is it one which is achieved without defeat. Jesus endures the most bitter of losses. He is executed as a common criminal with the approval of his own people and the religious establishment of that day. On the cross Jesus must have wondered, as we sometimes do, what went wrong along the way, how things might have been different, whether he was responsible for the failure.

The Gospel portrays Jesus as someone who loved with all his heart, someone who was as perfect a human being as one can imagine. Yet, even in this case, there were problems and heartaches, hostility and misunderstanding, envy and injury. Surely, Jesus did not want all this to happen to him.

It is no easy thing to be a human being. No one has an endlessly successful life, no matter how much it may seem to be so to outsiders.

~~~~~~~~~

There are other resources in the Church which are supportive.

The liturgy is one of the Church's finest moments, perhaps its most impressive deed.

We begin the liturgy by asking God for pardon, reflecting silently on our sins, praying for absolution and forgiveness. The assumption is that no one has come to the liturgy without fault, that we assemble as an imperfect people, that no one of our lives has been all it might have been or all we would have preferred.

The liturgy receives the gifts we bring, gifts of bread and wine, signs of poverty and insufficiency, symbols of the incompleteness of our lives. It is God and Christ who must make these gifts, and with them our lives, acceptable and worthy. We are to be transformed, as the gifts are, because we are not all we should be. Nor shall we ever reach that point without divine intervention.

The liturgy takes a broken people and proclaims their wholeness in Christ. It receives a wounded people and celebrates their healing in Christ. It embraces an impoverished people and announces their fulfillment in Christ.

The liturgy offers us the Presence of Christ in the Eucharistic ritual as nourishment for hungers in us we cannot satisfy, but also as a pledge for the goodness our lives have already achieved.

There are other resources in the Church. The Church offers us not only Gospel and liturgy but an impressive array of ministers. The Church is filled with caring people who are ready to help us when that is necessary and when we are willing. There are laity and sisters, deacons and brothers, priests and bishops whose lives and training are at our service.

Sometimes people complain about a disappointing experience with one or another minister. All professionals disenchant us at times. Some ministers are inadequate. But this is clearly not typical of all. The Church offers more assistance for recovery through its ministers than any one lifetime could exhaust.

~~~~~~~~

Every person recovers. There are, perhaps, no final failures. All of us eventually pass into the hands of God; we need not suppose that any human being is lost forever. Jesus lived and died for all of us; the grace of God misses no one; the Spirit dwells in every heart. We can never banish the Presence or the Image of God from our humanity. In us, Christ is wounded and recovers, is lost and found, is hungry and nourished, is lonely and loved.

We recover from almost everything in life. At the end, when life is most threatened and death itself imminent, when all seems lost and no human resource can rescue us, God takes us in hand and leads us to a homeland we never deserved and yet somehow knew was ours, a homeland where recovery happens no more because it is no longer possible to lose our way.

Reflection

The Prodigal Son

In the last reflection we considered the parable of the Good Samaritan. It may be fitting to focus our attention now on the Parable of the Prodigal Son. It is a wonderful story of recovery.

The parable begins as a young man is unkind to his father and leaves home. He abandons family and friends and goes to another country. He thinks only of what is due to him and not of what he can do for others, or of the harm his behavior causes. He breaks every bond which has held his life together.

Soon the young man discovers that money does not last forever and that superficial associates remain only as long as it suits their convenience. Others do to him what he had done to his father. He is left alone. He begins to starve to death. He is spiritually as well as physically malnourished.

It is then that he remembers his father's love and how readily his father forgave his faults in the past. In a moment of courage and humiliation, he recognizes his foolishness and the harm he has done. He begins the painful journey back, rehearsing the *words of a plea to his father that he be permitted to live and work on the farm, even though his father might never recognize him again as his son.*

The father receives him with so much love and affection, so much joy and exuberance, so much forgiveness and acceptance that the young man seems to be, not less, but even more than he was before he went away.

Jesus tells us, in the story, that the resources of love never run out, and that sometimes we are healed so deeply that it seems we have lost nothing along the way and gained more than we can handle.

Suffering

We enter life and leave it in tears. Jesus speaks of a daily cross in our lives. Buddhism tells us that all life suffers. The human journey is a painful one.

We need only visit a hospital or a nursing home, a slum or a hospice, a prison or a cancer ward to get a sense of the enormity of suffering in our world.

If we take into account battlefields and concentration camps, earthquakes and tornadoes, plane crashes and industrial accidents, the world seems to be a place of carnage. Unless one is blind and callous, the suffering of others reaches us. If it does not, we ourselves shall suffer soon enough. There is no escape.

Our objective, in this chapter, is the integration of the experience of suffering into the development of a contemporary spirituality.

We begin by observing that suffering, in all its forms, is an evil. No Christian has a right to choose it as a value in its own right. It is wrong to desire or pointlessly cause pain in another.

There are, unfortunately, Christians who believe that God is pleased with suffering. Such people suppose that God is less glorified in our joy than in our anguish. The assumption is made that sexual pleasure is somehow less holy than abstinence in each and every instance, that festivity is less sacred than isolation, that God receives us more readily in our injuries than in our wholeness.

It is almost impossible to describe how much harm has been done to human development and Christian spirituality by such attitudes. God is dishonored in such thinking and human life is diminished when we act on this outlook.

We have all heard people wonder how long God will let them get away with enjoying life. There is a sense in this that sooner or later God makes people pay for their love of life or their satisfaction with it. Success sometimes makes people anxious, because they believe that failure is our natural lot and that success accelerates or even causes the arrival of failure.

We have heard people say that God takes from us spouses and children if they are too beautiful or good.

When people actually suffer, they frequently conjecture that they deserved this, that God is punishing them and gratified with their agony, that this will make them more like Christ than anything else they have done.

There are even those who decide to inflict more pain on themselves than life brings them. And so the denial of the simple things the body needs to sustain itself or the human spirit needs to renew itself is sometimes suggested as a way to win God's love.

These approaches to the spiritual life are humorless and inhuman. They are sacrilege because they assault the holiest thing God made, namely, human life. They undervalue the splendor of the universe and they fail to take seriously God's promise that our lives and our world will be restored at the end of time. God, therefore, is committed to the glorification of our bodies, our world and all creation.

~~~~~~~~~

It is difficult to discern why it is that some people tend to prefer negative and distorted thinking. In some cases, people are frightened of their own humanity, ill at ease with their own emotions, insecure about their ability to let go without destroying themselves. In other cases, people feel a need to punish themselves for a guilt or a grief, a lack of love or a bad decision. It is supposed that if one suffers enough, the guilt may be absolved or, at least, given its due punishment. There is a hidden anger in this for not having been perfect.

There are those who believe in this twisted view of life because they have been taught this by parents or teachers, by pastors or religious people. God has been defined for them as angry and demanding, jealous and punishing, judgmental and condemnatory. Systems of theology to support this view have been formulated over the centuries; they propose that almost every human being is sent to

71

hell, that very few reach heaven, and then only if they have made their lives artificial, contrived and loveless.

All of this is grim beyond description.

Still others assume that God is pleased with holy wars against infidels and that the torture of heretics is justifiable. Some people actually pray for the suffering and death of supposed enemies of God and rejoice when calamity falls on them.

The point has been made. Thinking such as this is terrifying and cruel, barbarous and ugly.

We repeat. Suffering, in all its forms, is an evil. No Christian ought to choose it as a value in its own right.

~~~~~~~~~

If suffering is an evil, it is also an inevitability. If there is no escape from it, there need not be, nonetheless, any surrender to it.

One surrenders to suffering when one gives it undue attention, when one seeks it or desires it, when one fears it excessively or is preoccupied with it, when one becomes bitter or cynical, hopeless or indifferent about life because there is suffering in it.

The easiest way out of pain is not attending to it directly. The more we are focused on pain, the more its intensity is increased.

Suffering is not only inevitable; it is also an asset in our growth if it is addressed properly. Some of the distorted notions we alluded to earlier have a measure of truth in them, namely, that suffering serves a purpose and can even be helpful. Suffering does give us deeper insights and different responses to life. It enables us to relate to people and to ourselves in a new way.

One of the keys to a creative spirituality of suffering has something to do with its inevitability. If life always brings suffering with it, then it need never be sought but merely accepted. Every human life will have a measure of pain in it at different stages of the life process.

An acceptance of suffering gives us all the suffering we need, so to speak. The question is not whether we shall suffer or how much but what our attitude to it will be and what we shall make of it.

It is foolish to resent suffering, because this not only intensifies it but leads us to waste the opportunity to develop as Christians and as human beings. Resentment prompts us to inflict suffering on those around us, especially on those who love us most.

It is irrational and inhumane to strike out at those who come to heal us. We do this because there is no other way for us, it seems, to express our rage at the world for having been the world that it is. Such a response, needless to say, is neither creative nor welcome.

Early in the twentieth century, a spiritual principle was written about which one does not come across much anymore. It was called the sacrament of the present moment. It summed up in its few words a profound insight.

The sacrament of the present moment intends to make us aware of the meaningfulness of life and of the presence of God in each moment. It asks us not to look to the past and wish for something that was gone, or to the future to desire something which might not ever exist. It suggests, instead, that we live in the present moment, whether that moment be wonderful or frightening, and that we find in that moment something important to experience.

Each moment of life is sacramental because it reveals God to us and brings grace with it. Each moment makes us aware of who we are and enters into our life story. Some of these moments may be suffering moments, but these too teach us about the texture and quality of our lives and the nature and character of the universe we inhabit.

We know then that life brings more than enough suffering with it. We need not ever seek suffering for its own sake or inflict it on others. Suffering becomes a creative and contributive life experience when we allow life itself to determine the occasion and the intensity, the moment and the magnitude of the pain.

Every person suffers sooner or later. The poor suffer physical deprivation, but may experience stronger bonds with those they love and fewer illusions about life. The affluent suffer emotional distance from themselves and others, but receive more esteem and comfort. Those whose lives are socially unsuccessful suffer failure in the public order, but may be closer to their families and less infected with greed. The successful suffer stress, endless expectations for better performance and vicious competition, but they gain a sense of satisfaction with themselves and the acclaim of others.

There are trade-offs, so to speak. There are different assets and liabilities but, just possibly, the same degree of disadvantage.

It may be true, furthermore, that, in essence, we experience the same basic sufferings. No matter where we are in life or what happens to us we must suffer from our own limitations. No one of us achieves everything he or she wishes. We all deal with people who are indifferent to us or who do not like us, those who are hostile to us or insensitive to our suffering.

People we love and depend on die on us. We know that at some moment we shall die also.

We all suffer failure and inadequacy. Disease and injury afflict all of us. We all feel the sting of vanity and envy, of lust and gluttony, of anger and irresponsibility. We all have sins and regrets, guilts and shameful memories. We all are tempted on occasion to hurl the first stone at the beleaguered, anxious to create the impression that we are different from other sinners. We all have our judgmental and self-righteous moments.

We all worry about life more than we should. We all need to hear Christ tell us to be less anxious about food and clothing and to have a care for our hearts and our spirits.

We all have sleepless nights and restless days, discouraging mornings and lonely evenings.

Indeed, we may suffer not only in the same degree but from the same problems.

We need to address one other issue about suffering before we bring this chapter to a close.

If suffering must never be sought for its own sake, if life brings sufficient suffering for us all, is it ever useful to sustain pain for the achievement of something more significant than the pain? The answer to this question is clearly affirmative.

Pain is not merely something which comes to us as we passively await its arrival. It is also generated by the very act of living, by the choices we make and the goals we seek.

If one wishes to become an accomplished musician, an impressive athlete, a splendid writer, an unforgettable dancer, a noteworthy scholar, a famous physician, an excellent artist, one must suffer a great deal and endure discipline and deprivation. There is no easy way to excellence. This pain is not sought for its own sake, but it is pain nonetheless. It is sustained as an unfortunate and necessary consequence of the goal we seek.

If one wishes to be a loving spouse and a successful parent, a loyal friend and a reliable colleague, a trustworthy person and a committed believer, one must suffer, at times, the loss of one's own preferences and ease.

In the contexts we are considering, the suffering is diminished because the goal we strive for is worthwhile. Indeed, the goal, once achieved, seems to compensate abundantly for the sacrifice entailed while striving for it.

Jesus, on the cross, did not choose the pain. His crucifixion was a consequence of the life he had chosen to live. Jesus does not choose the suffering, only the life. Jesus does not choose the cross, only the love which makes the cross inevitable.

Reflection

Blessed by Agony

A scientist might seek to develop a serum which will save the life of a monkey and, later, of humans. The serum might prevent the monkey from suffering an agonizing death but require a painful series of injections.

The monkey would see the suffering as evil and consider the scientist an enemy. The monkey would choose not to endure the pain, which is necessary for its life, and will injure the scientist, if possible, rather than suffer this intrusion and assault. Yet the monkey would be destroying itself by its own resistance. It is rejecting a value but does not know this. If the monkey does not suffer, it will not live. Yet there is no way to explain this to the animal, no way to make the animal aware that it is being saved.

On a higher level of intelligence, all of this is clear. The scientist knows that the monkey is being cared for and that its own best interests are being served. On a lower level of understanding, it looks different.

Is it possible that on the higher level of God's intelligence and love, we are blessed by the very agony we would reject if we had the chance? Is it possible that what we often resist may be absolutely necessary for our own salvation?

Chapter Nine

Healing

In his novel *All the King's Men*, Robert Penn Warren, the American novelist and poet, observes that we live in a closed moral universe. By this he means that our ethical and human actions endure through all of history, affecting everyone.

This is a rather complex notion, but a wonderful and challenging one.

The assumption Warren is working with is the interconnectedness of human life.

Let us begin with a simple example. If a man comes home from work in an angry and depressed mood, he immediately affects the environment in the house he enters. His wife and children may be joyful because many good things happened to them through the day and they wish to share them with someone they love. As these two forces, anger and exuberance, meet each other, a change occurs.

We might take this example in two different directions. In the first instance, let us suppose that the anger is so severe and unrelenting that the man wishes to hear no good news. The enthusiasm of his family is an intrusion into the black mood he prefers. He is angry and he wishes no one to be content. He has been disturbed in his own life and he seeks to create disturbance in the lives of others, partly because he wants company in his misery, partly because he wishes others to pay for the treatment he has received.

In this case, the joyful environment is destroyed. An atmosphere of hostility and fear takes its place. The husband did not solve his problem but actually compounded and intensified it. The family has experienced something about anger and joy which it may never forget. Even if the family members forget, the experience will influence them in some permanent way. It may, for example, help generate in them an attitude that an angry man is to be feared, or that joy is not as important as rage, or that power matters more than happiness, or that exuberance is somehow out of order and has to justify its existence. The possibilities are endless. The children may observe how their mother handles this problem and take from it some notion about the role of women in society or the proper adult response to anger. That response may be retaliation or capitulation, pleading or silence, terror or indifference.

We need not continue the explanation, but one can see how the simple incident has ramifications almost beyond calculating.

~~~~~~~~

There is another direction in which our example might go. Let us suppose, instead, that the joy is so contagious and wholehearted, so irresistible in its appeal and delightful in its expression, that the man's anger is gone as soon as he enters the door. The man had intended to be downcast and heavyhearted, but he is so sensitive to his family and so open to influence from it that he becomes responsive almost instinctively. The two forces, hostility and happiness, have met, and the latter prevails.

A different lesson has now been learned. Anger is not as powerful as joy. One way to deal with anger is to surround it with contentment. Exuberance is not out of order; anger is. Anger needs to justify its existence and must take into account where people are.

The children may learn from their mother's attitude that the anger of their father is not a matter of no consequence, but neither is it the determining factor in how a family must behave. They may gather from this that women have enormous resources of strength and can meet the anger of men and overcome it. They may come to believe that the proper response to anger is not fear, but the assertion of other experiences which balance the anger and eventually prevail over it. The possibilities once again are endless. This simple example, taken now in another direction, has ramifications almost beyond calculating.

~~~~~~~~~

Now that we have this explanation before us, we can apply the principles of Robert Penn Warren to human behavior as such and to the present topic of healing.

Warren's point is that history is a constant process of interaction. Since we are connected to one another, each one has an influence on the other, even on those we have never met or never will meet.

An example, here, may help once again. Let us suppose that the angry father's mood prevails in the home. That evening when his children play with other children, they may be negative or aggressive. People who call his wife on the telephone may find that she is curt or, at least, indifferent. A visit the family might have planned to a lonely relative is postponed because no one feels up to it. One can see how others, beyond the family, are affected.

If this negativity prevails in other homes, the entire neighborhood develops an ugly and contentious air. When strangers enter it, they sense the unfriendliness. Love seems to be out of order in this part of the world, so it is withheld or expressed timidly.

If one can multiply these negative experiences, on the same day, around the world, one can see that they create a critical mass and that, all of a sudden, something happens which no one can explain and which no one seems to be responsible for, but to which, as we know, people have been contributing. A war may break out or a murder may occur; racism or heartless competition may win the day; the poor may be further oppressed or the needy may be even more neglected.

Of course, the reverse of all this may occur. The cumulative effect of goodness may create an environment in which generosity prevails and hostilities are dispelled. People may favor mercy and forgiveness over callousness and vengeance. The vulnerable may be supported and children given affection.

All of our actions and decisions make a difference. This is our central point. There is no such thing as an isolated human action, no such thing as an insignificant one.

The supposedly private human action has an effect on the kind of person we become. If we are kind in thought or action, even if no one but ourselves knows this, we become a kind person nonetheless. If we are seething with resentment and envy, even if no one but ourselves knows this, it takes its toll and we become a hostile person or, at least, a person who refuses to offer love and to be generous.

It seldom takes long for us to be with another person before we sense the kind of person we are meeting. We may not be able to put it into words, but we get a feeling that this person is trustworthy or treacherous.

There is, therefore, no isolated human action. It all counts. We may have done something as apparently inconsequential as being courteous with a clerk in a bank or a gas station attendant. We may have only given a greeting and shown respect to a sanitation worker or a janitor. It cost us so little that we hardly paid attention to the kindness. Yet the person who received the courtesy or the greeting feels more worthwhile as a result of this. If these small gestures are repeated by others, the recipients of all this begin to have a sense of respect for the lives they are living and the work that they do. If these people are married, the spouses and the children are now influenced by the enhanced self-respect.

There is no such thing as an insignificant human action. It all makes a difference.

~~~~~~~~~

As we reflect on these issues, we ought to sense how important each one of us is. We are responsible not only for ourselves but for the world we are making with others. We have a hand in it no matter how distant we seem to be from the supposed centers of power and influence.

Each of us makes a contribution to each day's cumulative aggregate of good and evil in the world. We are affected by the past in this process, since we inherit a certain kind of world and a specific set of parents and home environment which were set in place before we were born. We influence the future because the kind of world we hand on and the quality of our human life are passed on to those who come after us.

Each person helps change the balance. It is a beautiful and awesome truth.

~~~~~~~~~

When Jesus spoke to us of human life and its significance, he focused on simple and everyday occurrences. A shepherd loses a sheep; a woman misplaces a coin; a farmer sows seed; a fisherman hauls in a net of fish; a widow offers a small sum of money for the poor; a young man decides to return home to his father; a merchant buys a pearl; a disciple asks how to pray; a planter puts a mustard seed in the ground; a woman mixes yeast in flour; a landowner hires workers for his vineyard; a wedding party runs out of wine; a man invests his money; someone finds a treasure hidden in a field that belongs to no one; a person lights a lamp and puts it on a lampstand; a child runs into the arms of Jesus; a woman anoints his feet; a friend breaks bread for a guest; a woman sits to hear the Master; a lily of the field catches the eye of a storyteller and a sparrow finds food to eat on the ground.

There is an exquisite simplicity to the teaching of Jesus. Everything counts. Nothing is wasted. It all makes a difference.

Jesus is lyrically sensitive to the significance of every moment of life, to the meaningfulness of all that goes on each day in the history of the world.

When Jesus speaks of the Judgment at the end of time, he does so with simple eloquence once again. He employs the quiet gestures of life, those which escape the world's notice, as normative for our life and salvation.

Jesus cites tasks parents do every day as critical actions for the life of the world. He speaks of feeding those who are hungry and giving drink to the thirsty, of making others feel welcome and clothing those who are not dressed, of keeping the sick company and healing those who are injured. Jesus does not speak, at this decisive moment, of God being impressed with miracles and extraordinary success stories, of exotic contributions to human life or even of personal heroism. He tells us that a human life is made up of seemingly small deeds which are, ultimately, so significant that they are worth heaven.

Each person heals others and is healed. Every person is healed by those he or she never meets and heals those whose faces and names remain unknown. We are, indeed, one family together.

Reflection

Making the Ultimate Difference

If we are inclined to disbelieve the significance of our everyday actions on human history, an example may help.

Let us suppose that the only thing ever done by human beings in the world was to love. Let us suppose that no loveless action or thought, however slight, ever existed.

If this were the case, would not the character of life, even the shape of our bodies, be different? If we were never defensive, fearful, suspicious, we would not look the same. Nothing about our world would be as it is now. Animal and vegetative life, even in-

animate matter and, certainly, human history would be unimaginably changed.

On the contrary, if the only things we had ever done were loveless, everything we now see and experience would be otherwise. Indeed, life would have ceased on the planet because no one would have had the heart or the will to continue it.

Every simple action has its significance. As love is increased and multiplied, the world becomes a home, more fittingly, for all of us and the human heart rejoices. It is not a ruler or an army which makes the ultimate difference in our world. It is each and every one of us.

Chapter Ten

Community

No one wishes to be alone. People at times settle for this because there seems to be no hope for genuine community.

We have been made to be bonded. In this, each human person in God belongs to the other with a totality and completeness which cannot be replicated in the created order.

We have been made to belong.

We expend the greatest part of our lives and the most substantial of our efforts in a desire to connect. One of the most striking demonstrations of this is the intense interest people have in marriage.

Marriage is the most comprehensive and permanent human experience known. Its comprehensiveness includes all aspects of a person's life: emotional and physical, legal and financial, social and professional, health and sickness, life and death, love and happiness. The most moving and compelling words in any language are those associated with marriage and family: home, mother, father, son, daughter, child, sister, brother.

Marriage is not only comprehensive but permanent. No one begins a marriage envisioning its termination. Marriage is an area in which permanent commitment is expected and where anything less is a shock, a disappointment, a tragedy. People are not alarmed if friends move elsewhere or even if sons and daughters live at a distance from their parents. A couple living apart in separate locations is a sign that something is, quite likely, seriously wrong with this relationship. The permanency of marriage is a permanency which includes proximity.

Friendships may continue over a distance of miles; children remain connected even though they live across the country; but a marriage seldom survives physical separation and is almost always wounded by it.

Yet marriage, in spite of all its comprehensibility and permanence, in spite of all its demands on us and all the energy we choose to pour into it — marriage, in spite of all this, is something the human family continues to choose as the best opportunity for human happiness. Indeed, people often remarry after the death of a spouse or a divorce, repeatedly hoping that their original dreams will be realized.

Every married couple and all parents feel overwhelmed at times by how much is expected of them. And, yet, in most cases, they would not have it any other way. Living alone gives one enormous control over one's own life, it is true. It allows one to do more things and attend more to oneself. But people do not, by and large, see this as a desirable alternative.

Even when people remain unmarried, they choose, not to live alone, but to form friendships and to participate in religious or other communities which make considerable demands on them.

We give so much of ourselves, so endlessly in human history because we have been made to be bonded.

Community may well be the central focus and motivating factor behind all profound human action.

The Jewish philosopher Martin Buber said it well when he observed that "all meaning is in meeting." As we meet people on deeper and deeper levels of life, meaning becomes a permanent feature of our existence.

The Bible depicts God in the same way. God creates because community is the essence of God and because life and love are communicative. In Christ, God joins us in a community which brings together the human and the divine.

~~~~~~~~~

No life in the world creates life without connecting with it. Life is not generated at a distance. We behold in the origins of life the bonding which is life's very nature. This is true for all forms of life.

When we reach the human level, the beginnings of life are preceded by intense promises and commitments, by vows and selfgiving, by sacrifice and joy. It is always a disappointment when they are absent. People know that it is wrong for such pledges not to be there first.

Community happens so often and with such intensity that we take it for granted. The stories which seize our attention or that of the media are the failures in this regard. They are given prominence because they are less frequent than successful community, no matter how often they occur.

~~~~~~~~

The Eucharistic liturgy is an effective celebration of the fact that every person is community. As the Eucharist gathers the strands of wheat which go into the making of bread and all the grapes which go into formulating wine, it symbolizes the very community it assembles.

The Eucharist is an offering of bread which is broken but then transformed into new life, the life of Christ in communion with us and the life of ourselves in community. The Eucharist is a consecration of wine for the renewal and nourishment of love in and among us.

The Eucharist is a celebration open to all, even to those who do not yet know one another but have Christ in common and faith in God's presence to us.

The whole human family is invited to the celebration. The Church will not have completed its Eucharistic ministry to the world until all the world is part of the celebration.

The Christ who is the focal point of the ritual is the Christ who assures us that his life and death, his resurrection and Spirit are for all. Christ does not break bread for the few or offer wine to a restricted number. Christ is Lord of history, Savior of the world.

Christ asks us to love even our enemies before we come to the altar. In this sense, we bring them to the celebration in our reconciliation and harmony.

St. Paul goes on to remind us in the New Testament that in Christ we are neither Jew nor Gentile, slave nor free, male nor female.

The imperatives and possibilities of community are infinite. They embrace not only the entire human family but the divine family who is God. This belief in an eternal, human, divine, infinite, intimate global community is, perhaps, the single most exciting and profound truth in Christianity.

Human life, we are suggesting, is defined by relationship and community. This means that human life may not always be enriched by the use of that freedom which distinguishes us as human, or by that rationality which makes us a unique species. Human life seems, rather, to expand in direct proportion to the number and diversity of those with whom we are able to form significant relationships.

The Catholic doctrine of the Trinity defines each Person in terms of its relationship to the other Persons. The same is true of us. Our personalities are made substantial by the capacity we demonstrate to form wholehearted relationships. We have, indeed, been born to be bonded.

The more narrow and circumscribed the circle of those with whom we can relate, the less fully human we are. This does not mean that we may not choose to limit our close friendships to a very few, but that we are clearly a person able to relate to more if that would be necessary.

It is the capacity of Christ to appeal to all people in all ages from all cultures in all circumstances which reveals to us the completeness of his humanity and the nature of his relationship with God.

The themes of Eucharist remind us that no one of us has all the community life he or she needs. It is only by envisioning community as a catholic or universal experience, as a divine and Christic encounter, that one begins to consider a community which is adequate to us and even exceeds the requirements of the human heart.

Just as the Eucharistic bread is made whole from its numberless grains of wheat, so the human family is made entire from the incalculable people who compose it. The bread that is broken is broken so that it can be distributed to everyone. The brokenness is healed as all receive the bread and become the bread restored. As we enter into communion we become one body with one another and with Christ. The Eucharist assembles us and celebrates us.

The Eucharistic wine is shared with all from the crushed grapes which lose their individuality but not their distinctiveness of substance by becoming a common cup for all. The wine is divided and diminished so that it might become our life, a common life which excludes no one and includes Christ.

When Christ, describing judgment asks that the hungry be fed and the thirsty given drink, two things seem to be in his mind. In the first instance, Christ intends the physical nourishment of the human family. Just as a family becomes a family by sharing common meals, so the human family is to offer food to all in generosity and with respect for personal dignity.

Few exclusions are more painful than the refusal to serve a child or guest while others are being fed from the common table. We wound not only them but ourselves by such a denial. The same is true of the human family. If we exclude anyone, we injure everyone even though we do not always realize this at the time. The world is the common table for all God's children. And so, Christ asks that all be nourished and that no one be turned away.

In the second instance, however, Christ intends something else. He tells us, on another occasion, that we do not live by bread alone. He asks us, furthermore, to pray for daily bread. We need, therefore, to be fed by the Word of God and by the love we give one another. We need to be nourished not only in community but by the very community to which we belong. A father gives his children not only bread but all the words of his life and the spirit of his love as well. Otherwise it is not a father's bread which is being offered and these are not truly his children. Children are not a father's obligation; they are his community.

It is, therefore, community we seek as we take bread and break it, as we share food and are nourished by it. The bread is ourselves because it contains not only our hearts and our devotion, not only our families and community, but even our Christ and our God.

This bread and wine also represent the broken body of Jesus on the cross, a symbol of all our deaths in one death; they remind us, furthermore, of the risen body of Christ from the empty tomb, a symbol of all our lives in one life.

Every person is community because all of us have been made for one another by a God who made all of us for Christ.

Reflection

Three Simple Words

The etymology of three simple words says it all.

To have "compassion" is to feel someone else's pain as our own. To find a "companion" is, literally, to discover someone who breaks bread with us. To experience "communion" is to encounter someone with whom we are so thoroughly united that we are, in a sense, one person.

Each of us is meant to be a compassionate companion of all those who are in communion with us as a human family.

Christ becomes in the Eucharist a compassionate God who breaks bread for us as a companion so that there might be communion between us.

Community is another way of saying communion. And communion is what the Eucharist and human life were meant to be when first they were made.

Chapter Eleven

Christ

Whom is it we seek in all the pathways and byways of life? What is it we desire to accomplish in all our striving and searching? Is there a common goal the entire human family reaches for, since so many of the hopes and dreams seem the same?

The spiritual life is not a strange and alien life, one removed from what everyone needs and wants, one sustained only by artificial and contrived systems. The spiritual life is, in reality, another way of defining or labeling the human journey itself. We have all been made for the same things and we all strive for the same objectives.

When people are asked what they want most in life, they tend to respond superficially at first. The question is often raised in a half-serious, half-playful mood. Even if it is a genuine request, it may be made by someone we do not really know or are not certain we can fully trust. The question, after all, makes us vulnerable. And so, people response frivolously. They know that the question needs an answer and that it has haunted them in their own lives. But they will be reticent or oblique if the wrong person makes the inquiry at the wrong time.

People, therefore, give answers which are expected, answers which are so common that they protect their vulnerabilities. They speak of money or power, youth or beauty, fame or pleasure.

Such answers are not, in themselves, bad answers. They are symbols of deeper needs. The need for money or power is a manifestation of insecurity and a hope that security might be gained by wealth or influence. The need for youth and beauty or fame has something to do with a disappointment with the level of our acceptance by others and an assumption that attractiveness may win us attention, without our having to make a significant effort. The need for pleasure is a symptom of dissatisfaction with our lives.

These superficial and common answers mask needs for security, acceptance, satisfaction or other requirements.

~~~~~~~~

We also sense, nonetheless, that money and power have only limited ability to make us secure. There have been too many stories over the years of the unhappiness and greed, the addictions and betrayals, the callousness and the arrogance of the wealthy and the powerful for us to believe that security comes automatically with such assets. These advantages do provide comfort but they also create disadvantages.

We know that beauty creates excitement, but it also attracts people to us for reasons which are not always satisfying. We have all been young and we are aware that youth is a wonderful but also a terrifying experience. Maturity often brings a tranquility and self-acceptance which compensate for the perplexities and problems of youth.

Fame also has its benefits and liabilities. It is possible to be recognized everywhere but to suffer loneliness. Fame may compel us to repeat the role or the expectation which brought us renown, but to hide the true self we would rather reveal. Fame creates attention but wears thin after a while. It brings curiosity when we seek acceptance. After a time, we are harassed by fame and made brittle because so much is demanded of us. We begin to prefer privacy with a few who accept us with no reference to fame.

Pleasure provides satisfaction in small and transient doses. It does not forever ward off isolation or satisfy the needs of the human heart. It has its limits, set by biology and the human spirit. In large doses, pleasure becomes tedious, and then painful.

~~~~~~~~~

The superficial answers we have surveyed disclose needs which are not superficial.

When people are with friends or lovers, however, they speak differently. They might begin with the same list: money and power, beauty and youth, fame and pleasure. They often smile or laugh as they repeat these goals. They do so, I believe, partly because they believe these objectives are unattainable, partly because they suspect such advantages may be foolish or fraudulent.

If they speak their heart, they then move on to state other objectives, objectives which no longer lead them to smile or shrug their shoulders. Now they may affirm that they want love, more than anything else, from life. Or they might even name those whose love is important. They might tell us that they wished their children loved them more or that they loved their spouses better. They might confess that they never received from a parent the love they needed, or that they are guilty for not having loved a parent sufficiently in return. At this point, there are no smiles.

The people we imagine in this scenario may tell us that they wished someone would have assured them that their lives were not pointless, that they had some meaning, that they made the world a little better, that they might be remembered with gratitude. We are now dealing with the hunger for significance.

We might hear about the fear of death and the terror that suffering instills. We may be told that they do not want to see their loved ones suffer and die, that they would willingly take their place if it would stop the pain, that, in any case, they fear they may not be up to the task of facing properly all the agonies they envision in the process of dying. We are now being told about the need for life.

Some final references might be made to peace for

the world and for themselves. A sense of connectedness with others may lead them to wish that someday there will be justice in the world and no more weapons, even if they are not here to see this. They may tell us how much they want a world with no poverty for anyone, a world in which no children are neglected or die, a world in which hunger and homelessness are banished.

The vision becomes moving and profound.

Love and meaning, life and peace, a world that has found its heart, a human family that has recovered its soul. In such memories and hopes, in such desires and longings, there are tears and a need to look away from the questioner because the feelings are now deep and the vulnerability is painful.

At this moment, to speak of money and power is banal. Money and power cannot bring about such a world. Beauty, youth and fame seem out of place and inadequate. To suggest that pleasure can bring this world about is inept and embarrassing.

~~~~~~~~

There are deep spiritual hungers in the human heart and they need to be addressed. Life is too short and tragic, too sacred and substantive for us to trivialize it with banalities.

Our culture may lull us into a sense that we must have money and power and beauty and youth and fame and pleasure to be happy. All we need, however, is for a friend to ask us about what is best in life, and we know that these are not priorities for us.

They attract us because they are not bad in themselves, or because we do not know how else to have our needs met. But each of us is more than all that.

~~~~~~~~~

We search for someone credible to address our spiritual hunger. We require someone we trust to make believable promises to us. We look for a source of love and meaning, of life and peace, of justice and compassion.

The Gospel identifies Jesus Christ as such a person.

One reason why some hesitate to accept this answer is because the Gospel is sometimes presented artificially or by people who have neither Christ's interests nor ours at heart. We may sense we need the Gospel but we can do without "churchiness." We prefer to be part of the world, fully immersed in it and yet not of it nor trapped by it. We want to belong to ourselves and not be forced into a church's or preacher's agenda for us.

We may need not only to hear the Gospel proclaimed in public but, more importantly, to sit down alone with the Gospel, to read it and pray over it, to become contemplative and silent.

There is, perhaps, no one who emerges as a more powerful symbol of love than Christ. All the things awaited with love are at the heart of his teaching and are present in the way he lived. We meet there astonishing forgiveness and abundant mercy. And, of course, the commandment that we love one another as he has loved us.

We meet in Christ someone who offers us life on levels which are not superficial and who promises that life will never end. The Gospel portrays Christ as someone who overcomes death even in this world, and who does this in so convincing a manner that the world at large is willing to consider, only in the case of Jesus, the accomplishment of this apparent impossibility.

We meet in Christ someone who seems to meet us in all the places where meaning is most at issue in our lives. Christ tells us that God actually knows us and cares for us personally. He offers his own life and death for us. He teaches the significance of all the things we do and the irreplaceable value of each and every life.

And Christ talks of peace, of a peace which is more than the whole world can give us, a peace which surpasses understanding and reaches the human heart with its fullness.

Christ promises a world in which all people will be safe, a world which achieves a moment when all the tears will be gone, all the bruises healed, all the death vanquished, all the faces and names of everyone known and valued.

Christ asks us to put no ultimate trust in money or power, in beauty or youth, in fame or pleasure. We know this, in our heart of hearts, to be wisdom and grace and even truth itself.

~~~~~~~~

It may well be that the one we have been seeking in all the pathways and byways of life is the Christ who seems to be present in all of us and identified with each of us. It may well be that what we have hoped for most in our striving and searching is the kind of world Christ represents and brings to pass, for himself and all of us. It may well be that the whole world is impressed with Christ because Christ has spoken for all of us and even, perhaps, is all of us.

In the previous chapter we spoke of community as a way of completing ourselves in the Eucharistic sharing. The Eucharist, however, is not only our assembly, with Christ in our midst. It is also our way of becoming Christ by being nourished through him. Just as food becomes ourselves in a marvelous and remarkable manner, so the bread and wine of Christ's presence becomes our presence as well. In the Eucharist, Christ gives us his Spirit and we become members of his Body.

If we are, in a sense, Christ, then each of us is bread and wine for all of us. If we are Christ, then we have already in us the love and meaning, the life and peace, the dreams we have dreamt most often for the world and ourselves and the possibility of their permanent accomplishment. Hope passes into fulfillment, dream into reality, individualism into community. All of a sudden, the Christ we have sought all life long under different names and in unknown ways is each of us and all of us.

Reflection

Fulfilled in Christ

Jesus at the Last Supper tried to convince the disciples that they were his friends. They were not those who would only learn of Christ but those who were so identified with him that he would not part from them. The identity was symbolized in the bread and wine, in the washing of the feet and in the presence of the Spirit.

Jesus spoke of going away only to prepare a home for them in heaven. Now, they had become so much a part of each other that Christ could not be complete without them and they could not be fulfilled without him.

Chapter Twelve

Gratitude And Grace

We have come a long way together.

There are still steps to take on this journey.

In earlier chapters, we alluded to our communal bonding with all men and women. It is this sense of our oneness which makes justice and peace such an urgent concern for all of us.

We would have missed the point of this book if we could now be complacent about the inequity and the turmoil in the human family. In a world of abundance, the fact that people starve to death every day is a scandal and a horror. Of all forms of death, starvation is one of the most grisly. To have a child die in our arms weeping for bread is a trauma for anyone whose humanity is still intact. To know that this tragedy was preventable adds to the pain and the pity.

A Christian is someone raised with the idea that bread is to be broken and shared. In every Eucharist, we enter into communion with one another. No one claims the bread or the wine as his or her own.

107

Rather, the bread is for the community and the wine is for one another.

If we enter deeply into this ritual, we discover that we have some restless days and anxious nights. For we know, do we not, that the daily bread of this planet is broken for too few and shared for a limited number. As we are nourished, others die. As our hands are filled, the hands of the poor are empty and lifeless.

This book does not offer a strategy for justice or a program for economic equity in the world. Such a task is beyond its scope.

And yet, how can we draw our writing to a close without a word on behalf of all those who literally have nothing? I have seen the slums of Calcutta and Hong Kong, the misery of Brazil and Haiti. The children who died on the streets of other cities were not less worthy of life than the children I hold in my arms in America. Every child is a privilege. When a child dies needlessly, I become fatherless and an orphan. As a child turns aside in tears and dies, a grace passes from our world that nothing can replace.

Justice is not an empty concept. It is as concrete as a child's pain, as touching as the hands of those who plead for life.

The world needs work for all those who desire to live a life of dignity. It requires racial equality, gender fairness, ethnic equity. The world must provide lumber and stones for those who are homeless, wool and cotton for those who are naked, healing for those with wounds, education for those whose minds are eager for enlightenment.

We who love Christ must not allow him, of all people, to have no bread. We must not send Christ naked to his death again. This time we must find room for him in the inn. Christ must have oil for his wounds and justice from us, at the very least.

~~~~~~~~

The same Christ who is the bread of life is also Prince of Peace.

As long as men and women have lived on this planet, they have dreamed of peace. One day, all the swords will become plowshares, all the weapons will be left unused, all the bloodshed and violence will end. We have never lost this dream. If we do, our humanity will go with it.

And so we who have read this book and professed faith in Christ must not go away without a resolution. We must resolve that we shall turn the angry words into forgiveness and replace hostility with tolerance. War begins in the human heart and must come to an end there. The heart was made for love. Belligerence destroys the heart first of all and then attacks life itself.

~~~~~~~~

We have come a long way together.

We are summoned, in the beginning, by a sense of vocation and destiny. We have come to believe, on this journey, that God cared about us enough to give us meaning. We have a part to play in a scheme so grand, in a plan so sacred that we become silent as we ponder it.

We learned on our journey together that each of us was a liturgy in his or her own right, that the themes at the heart of the sacramental system were the themes at the heart of human life. There is no way to be fully human without being also, in some way, Christian, no way to be authentically Christian without becoming genuinely human. And so realities pass into one another on our journey, and convergence and unity happen everywhere.

We began the journey brought into life as a creative people, made unpredictable and reliable at one and the same time. Each of us is the world itself, not only in terms of how much the world is summed up in us but also in terms of how much we belong to the world and are affected by it even as we influence its development.

We took others steps on the journey. We are confirmed as sacred and invited to be contemplative. We are children of the Spirit.

Contemplation enables us to realize the creativity and the gifts we have been given.

In these initial steps of the journey, we were defined. We emerged as a creative and sacred people, made for the world and contemplation.

~~~~~~~~~

There were other turns in the road, other paths to travel. Now that the journey was advanced, we learned about the need to give ourselves and discovered the joy we found in doing this.

We began to give life and found that life was given back abundantly. Nothing seemed more wonderfully satisfying than to know that we were able to bring people into life and that there was more life on this planet because we were here. We gave life because we had to, and because it was glorious to do so, and because we would not have it any other way.

The life we were responsible for was life to which we felt a sense of responsibility. And so, God-like, we loved what we created and we were exhilarated when all we made loved us in return. Love became the greatest of our doings, the finest of our achievements, the substance and fulfillment of all our dreams.

There were other imperatives. We felt the marriage themes of life and love take flesh in us, but we also became aware of ordination themes of consecration and liturgy. Every person is a sacrament, revealing life and, eventually, God in an extraordinary and humbling manner.

More happened. Together we became not only sacrament but Church. The Church was less a place or a structure than it was the human heart at one state of its development. The Church was the human heart in its encounter with God. The Church became for us the themes of life and love endlessly repeated as sacraments in a community of grace and glory. Every human being was, in a sense, priest and spouse, sacrament and Church.

The journey was not only bright with promise and beautiful in its each and every moment. It was also troubling at times and discouraging. We failed and doubted ourselves, learning from the failure that all did not depend on us, finding in the failure that there was always a way to recover and there were always people committed to making this happen.

In these sometimes stumbling steps on the journey, we learned about failure and suffering. But we were supported by recovery and healing. The entire world emerged as a system in which resources to restore us were set in place and continually operative.

~~~~~~~~

We considered, finally, the completion of the journey. Here, Eucharistic themes of community and Christ became dominant.

We were made for community, and therefore we rejoice in it. We might be anxious at times to belong and fearful that we might be isolated or neglected, forgotten or dismissed. We learned that there are more communities in life which have a place for us than we could ever join. We can only be lost and fail to participate if we choose to allow this to happen.

At the center of our best efforts at community is Christ. Christ was a companion on the journey even when we did not know this, a Christ who was present from beginning to end, a Christ who offered us at last the very things we wanted but had feared we could not have.

And so each of our lives is worthy of a Eucharistic celebration because Christ is at issue in all of us. We are saved, with community all around us and Christ in our hearts, with our deepest needs met and the journey revealed as a sacred and liturgical experience. How could we not sing and worship?

Gratitude and grace. All of it was gratitude and grace. All of it was gift and thanksgiving. How could we have had so little faith in the venture? Why did we not love more on the way?

In any case, we end the journey as it had been started, with an answer to a vocation and a summons. Now, however, the calling is to completion. God never left us without life and love at any step along the way. God gave us the world and the sacred, the Church and the sacraments, healing and recovery, companions and compassion, communion and contemplation, all the human values and even the divine.

In contemplative and sacred wonder, fully recovered from our failures and healed of all wounds, in a community with Christ and creativity with one another, we sing a song of gratitude and find that all is grace. It was all gratitude and grace. When we know this, there is nothing else to know.

Other Resurrection Press Publications

Transformed by Love. The Way of Mary Magdalen. Sr. Margaret Magdalen, CSMV. Foreword by Jean Vanier.

Drawing from Mary Magdalen's experience, the author shows the vital role of transformed passion as a God-given and essential part of the Christian life. Each chapter is based on an aspect of Mary's transformation through love, but widens out to embrace life experiences that touch us all: passion, penitence, fervor, darkness in prayer, freedom. $5.95

Give Them Shelter. Responding to Hunger and Homelessness. Michael Moran.

The amazing story of the Interfaith Nutrition Network's soup kitchens and emergency shelters, the network of volunteers and donations which maintain The INN, and the breakdown of the underlying causes of hunger and homelessness. Written with wisdom, humor and compassion by the Director of The INN. $5.95

Behold the Man. Seven Meditations on the Passion, Death and Resurrection of Jesus. Judy Marley, S.F.O.

These meditations on the mental suffering of Jesus during his last days on earth take us on a journey from the poignant fellowship of the Last Supper to Golgotha, and beyond that to resurrection triumph. A passport to an unforgettable journey with Jesus. $2.95

60-minute audiocassette:

Divided Loyalties. Church Renewal Through a Reformed Priesthood. Dr. Anthony T. Padovano.

In this thought-provoking and timely reflection on today's Church, Dr. Padovano exhorts us to fashion a new Church. His keen historical perspectives, powerful analogies and loving example of service will inspire you to make the Church a credible Church where hope, truth and mercy prevail. $6.95

Available from your bookseller or directly from Resurrection Press, P.O. Box 248, Williston Park, NY 11596. (Add $1 for the first item and 50¢ for each additional item for shipping.)